The Defence of The Bride & Other Poems by Anna Katharine Green

Anna Katharine Green was born in Brooklyn, New York on November 11th, 1846.

Anna's initial ambition was to be a poet. However that path failed to ignite any significant interest and she turned to fiction writing. She published her first—and most famous work in 1878—'The Leavenworth Case'. Wilkie Collins praised it and it sold extremely well.

It led to Anna writing 40 novels and to becoming known as 'the mother of the detective novel.'

In helping to shape the genre she brought many other innovations including a series detective: her main character was detective Ebenezer Gryce of the New York Metropolitan Police Force, but in three novels he is assisted by the nosy society spinster Amelia Butterworth, another innovation and a prototype for Miss Marple, Miss Silver and others.

She also invented the 'girl detective': in the character of Violet Strange, a debutante with a secret life as a sleuth. Anna's other innovations included the now familiar dead bodies in libraries, newspaper clippings as "clews," the coroner's inquest, and expert witnesses. Yale Law School once used her books to demonstrate how damaging it can be to rely on circumstantial evidence.

Her career was now well advanced and she was much admired.

On November 25, 1884, Green married the actor and stove designer, and later noted furniture maker, Charles Rohlfs, who was seven years her junior. They had three children; Rosamund, Roland and Sterling.

Although Anna was a progressive she did not approve of many of her feminist contemporaries, and was opposed to women's suffrage.

On November 25, 1884, Anna married the actor and noted furniture maker, Charles Rohlfs, who was seven years her junior. They had three children; Rosamund, Roland and Sterling.

Anna Katharine Green died on April 11, 1935 in Buffalo, New York, at the age of 88.

Index of Contents

The Defence of the Bride

He was coming from the altar when the tocsin rang alarm,
With his fair young wife beside him, lovely in her bridal charm;
But he was not one to palter with a duty, or to slight
The trumpet-call of honor for his vantage or delight.

Turning from the bride beside him to his stern and martial train,
From their midst he summoned to him the brothers of Germain;
At the word they stepped before him, nine strong warriors brave and true,
From the youngest to the eldest, Enguerrand to mighty Hugh.

"Sons of Germain, to your keeping do I yield my bride to-day.
Guard her well as you do love me; guard her well and holily.
Dearer than mine own soul to me, you will hold her as your life,
'Gainst the guile of seeming friendship and the force of open strife."

"We will guard her," cried they firmly; and with just another glance
On the yearning and despairing in his young wife's countenance,
Gallant Beaufort strode before them down the aisle and through the door,
And a shadow came and lingered where the sunlight stood before.

Eight long months the young wife waited, watching from her bridal room
For the coming of her husband up the valley forest's gloom.
Eight long months the sons of Germain paced the ramparts and the wall,
With their hands upon their halberds ready for the battle-call.

Then there came a sound of trumpets pealing up the vale below,
And a dozen floating banners lit the forest with their glow,
And the bride arose like morning when it feels the sunlight nigh,
And her smile was like a rainbow flashing from a misty sky.

But the eldest son of Germain lifting voice from off the wall,
Cried aloud, "It is a stranger's and not Sir Beaufort's call;
Have you ne'er a slighted lover or a kinsman with a heart
Base enough to seek his vengeance at the sharp end of the dart?"

"There is Sassard of the Mountains," answered she without guile,
"While I wedded at the chancel, he stood mocking in the aisle;
And my maidens say he swore there that for all my plighted vow,
They would see me in his castle yet upon Morency's brow."

"It is Sassard and no other then," her noble guardian cried;
"There is craft in yonder summons," and he rung his sword beside.
"To the walls, ye sons of Germain! and as each would hold his life
From the bitter shame of falsehood, let us hold our master's wife."

"Can you hold her, can you shield her from the breezes that await?"
Cried the stinging voice of Sassard from his stand beside the gate.
"If you have the power to shield her from the sunlight and the wind,
You may shield her from stern Sassard when his falchion is untwined."

"We can hold her, we can shield her," leaped like fire from off the wall,
And young Enguerrand the valiant, sprang out before them all.
"And if breezes bring dishonor, we will guard her from their breath,
Though we yield her to the keeping of the sacred arms of Death."

And with force that never faltered, did they guard her all that day,
Though the strength of triple armies seemed to battle in the fray,
The old castle's rugged ramparts holding firm against the foe,
As a goodly dyke resisteth the whelming billow's flow.

But next morning as the sunlight rose in splendor over all,
Hugh the mighty, sank heart-wounded in his station on the wall,
At the noon the valiant Raoul of the merry eye and heart,
Gave his beauty and his jestings to the foeman's jealous dart.

Gallant Maurice next sank faltering with a death wound 'neath his hair,
But still fighting on till Sassard pressed across him up the stair.
Generous Clement followed after, crying as his spirit passed,
"Sons of Germain to the rescue, and be loyal to the last!"

Gentle Jaspar, lordly Clarence, Sessamine the doughty brand,
Even Henri who had yielded ne'er before to mortal hand;
One by one they fall and perish, while the vaunting foemen pour
Through the breach and up the courtway to the very turret's door.

Enguerrand and Stephen only now were left of all that nine,
To protect the single stairway from the traitor's fell design;
But with might as 'twere of thirty, did they wield the axe and brand,
Striving in their desperation the fierce onslaught to withstand.

But what man of power so godlike he can stay the billow's wrack,
Or with single-handed weapon hold an hundred foemen back!
As the sun turned sadly westward, with a wild despairing cry,
Stephen bowed his noble forehead and sank down on earth to die.

"Ah ha!" then cried cruel Sassard with his foot upon the stair,
"Have I come to thee, my boaster?" and he whirled his sword in air.
"Thou who pratest of thy power to protect her to the death,
What think'st thou now of Sassard and the wind's aspiring breath?"

"What I think let this same show you," answered fiery Enguerrand,
And he poised his lofty battle-ax with sure and steady hand;
"Now as Heaven loveth justice, may this deathly weapon fall
On the murderer of my brothers and th' undoer of us all."

With one mighty whirl he sent it; flashing from his hand it came,
Like the lightning from the heavens in a whirl of awful flame,
And betwixt the brows of Sassard and his two false eyeballs passed,
And the murderer sank before it, like a tree before the blast.

"Now ye minions of a traitor if you look for vengeance, come!"
And his voice was like a trumpet when it clangs a victor home.
But a cry from far below him rose like thunder upward,
"Nay! Let them turn and meet the husband if they hunger for the fray."

O the yell that sprang to heaven as that voice swept up the stair,
And the slaughter dire that followed in another moment there!
From the least unto the greatest, from the henchman to the lord,
Not a man on all that stairway lived to sheath again his sword.

At the top that flame-bound forehead, at the base that blade of fire⊠
'Twas the meeting of two tempests in their potency and ire.
Ere the moon could falter inward with its pity and its woe,
Beaufort saw the path before him unencumbered of the foe.

Saw his pathway unencumbered and strode up and o'er the floor,
Even to the very threshold of his lovely lady's door,
And already in his fancy did he see the golden beam
Of her locks upon his shoulder and her sweet eyes' happy gleam:

When behold a form upstarting from the shadows at his side.
That with naked sword uplifted barred the passage to his bride;
It was Enguerrand the dauntless, but with staring eyes and hair
Blowing wild about a forehead pale as snow in moonlit glare.

"Ah my master, we have held her, we have guarded her," he said,
"Not a shadow of dishonor has so much as touched her head.
Twenty wretches lie below there with the brothers of Germain,
Twenty foemen of her honor that I, Enguerrand, have slain.

"But one other foe remaineth, one remaineth yet," he cried,
"Which it fits this hand to punish ere you cross unto your bride.
It is I, Enguerrand!" shrieked he;"and as I have slain the rest,
So I smite this foeman also!"⊠ and his sword plunged through his breast.

O the horror of that moment!"Art thou mad my Enguerrand?"

Cried his master, striving wildly to withdraw the fatal brand.
But the stern youth smiling sadly, started back from his embrace,
While a flash like summer lightning, flickered direful on his face.

"Yes, a traitor worse than Sassard;" and he pointed down the stair,
"For my heart has dared to love her whom my hand defended there.
While the others fought for honor, I by passion was made strong,
Set your heel upon my bosom for my soul has done you wrong.

"But," and here he swayed and faltered till his knee sank on the floor,
Yet in falling turned his forehead ever toward that silent door;
"But your warrior hand my master, may take mine without a stain,
For my hand has e'er been loyal, and your enemy is slain."

Through The Trees

If I had known whose face I'd see
    Above the hedge, beside the rose;
If I had known whose voice I'd hear
    Make music where the wind-flower blow's,⬚
I had not come; I had not come.

If I had known his deep "I love "
    Could make her face so fair to see;
If I had known her shy "And I"
    Could make him stoop so tenderly,⬚
I had not come; I had not come.

But what knew I? The summer breeze
    Stopped not to cry "Beware! beware!"
The vine-wreaths drooping from the trees
    Caught not my sleeve with soft "Take care!"
And so I came, and so I came.

The roses that his hands have plucked,
    Are sweet to me, are death to me;
Between them, as through living flames
    I pass, I clutch them, crush them, see!
The bloom for her, the thorn for me.

The brooks leap up with many a song⬚
    I once could sing, like them could sing;
They fall; 'tis like a sigh among
    A world of joy and blossoming.⬚
Why did I come? Why did I come?

The blue sky burns like altar fires⬚
    How sweet her eyes beneath her hair!
The green earth lights its fragrant pyres;

The wild birds rise and flush the air;
God looks and smiles, earth is so fair.

But ah! 'twixt me and yon bright heaven
   Two bended heads pass darkling by;
And loud above the bird and brook
   I hear a low "I love," "And I "▢
And hide my face. Ah God! Why? Why?

The Nightingale

And now soft night hath ta'en her seat on high,
Outbreathing balmy peace o'er all the land;
Silent in sleep the dimpled meadows lie
Like tired children soothed by mother's hand.
Throughout the valley hums the zephyr bland,
Charming the roses from their passionate dreams,
To hear the wild and melancholy streams
Pulse to the waving of its mystic wand;
While large and low eans down the mellow moon,
Whose whitely blazing urn doth make a silver noon.

But hark! what heavenly sound is this that now
Steals like a dream adown the fragrant vale,
Or like a thought across a maiden's brow,
That brings a lambent flush upon the pale?
It is the heart-song of the nightingale,
Which yearns forever upward in a mist
Of subtle sadness, clouding all who list,
With softened shadows of her secret ail;
And now so purely fills the silence clear,
Great Nature seems to hush her beating heart to hear.

The Tower Of Bouverie

"Fill the horn unto the brim!"
Cried the Lord of Bouverie;
"Courtier gay and warrior grim,
All who feast this day with me,
Whatsoever his degree,
Fill ye, fill to Bouverie!"
Bounteously the red wine ran;
Up they rose unto a man.

"Here's to triumph in the wars!
Here's to pleasure in our halls!
Here's to Turkish scimitars
Hanging on our English walls!

Here's to peace! and here's to see
Ere another week can flee,
A fair bride in Bouverie!"

Loud the answering shout goes up,
Man by man they drain the cup.
Monteith's earl and Duffield's lord,
Hamon of the bloody sword,
Even gentle Hugh of Dee,
And the squire of Enderby,
All, all drink to Bouverie.

All, say I? Hold, I am wrong;
One there was amid that throng,
One, just one, who started back,
Tossed to heaven his tresses black,
Would not drink to Bouverie:
One alone; ah, who is he
Dares slight pledge of Bouverie?

Is it stalwart Clarimaux
Of the giant arm and knee?
Holbert's earl, or scornful Vaux?
Jasper, prince of chivalry?
No, ah no; too young to be
One amongst such warriors free,
Neither lord nor chieftain he.

Rupert, then, of careless eye,
Reckless if he live or die?
Eustace, loving more his wit
Than the head producing it?
No, ah no, not one of these
With their jests and mummeries,
But a simple squire, no more,
Is the man who thus before
All the world dares Bouverie.
Just a simple squire, but oh,
What a fire his glances show!
What a gesture of command
Speaks in his uplifted hand
As he puts the beaker back,
Crying, "Bring no pledge to me!
Though the castle fall in wrack
Drink I no such mockery."

But the master with a bound
Grasps the slighted goblet round,
Draws his sword, and, "Drink or die!"
Cries aloud and threateningly,
Whirling up his blade on high.

From the goblet's tempting rim
To the falchion fierce and grim,
Quickly passed the stripling's eye.
Sweet is life to youthful hearts,
Chill the dreaded angel's darts;
Sweet is life and harsh is death,
Sweet the sunshine's fervid breath,
And the winds that round us fly.
In his hand he took the cup◻
Like a wave the cry leaps up◻
"Long live Bouverie to wield
Sword of might in hall and field!"

"Pledge and drink!" the baron cried.
"I will pledge," the youth replied;
And his eye flashed like a star
In the gulf of night afar.
"I will pledge;" and o'er his head
Raised the goblet gleaming red.

"Here's to triumph in the wars!
Here's to pleasure in our halls!
Here's to Turkish scimitars
Hanging on our English walls!

Here's to peace! and here's to see
Ere another week can flee,
A dead bride in Bouverie."

Clanging loud the goblet falls;
He has flung it at the walls,
And a silence like a pall
For a moment shrouds the hall.
Then a sudden cry of "Shame!"
Curls about him like a flame,
And "Who art thou?" shriek they all,
"Devil's imp or dog abhorred,
Hissing snake or church-yard ghoul,
That you come to scare the soul
Of the baron at his board?"
But the master cries aloud
With a glance and gesture proud,
"Whosoever he may be,
Fool or devil, by my sword
He shall straight undo that word,
Or I am no Bouverie!"

"By thy life and by thy sword
But I'll not undo my word!
Gentle dame and fair is she,

Surly lord and spiteful he;
Better see her beauty dead
Than such sorrow on her head!
Die, then, lady, die and be
Laid to rest in Bouverie,
Ere such evil come to thee!"

O, to slay him where he stood!
Eager flashed an hundred swords,
But the baron's potent mood
Held them back withouten words.
"Demon imp or earth-born fool,
Scum of hell or Paynim's tool,
What to you is he or she?
What to you her misery?
What, the maid of Bouverie? "

"What the shrine is to the priest,
What his shield is to the knight,
What the sun is to the east,
Wearying for the morning light;
What the star is to the sea,
To my humbleness is she,
Glorious star of Bouverie!"

"O ho!" then the baron cried,
With a laugh of scornful pride,
"By the mem'ry of our sires,
But he loves, this squire of squires,
Loves our child of Bouverie!"
"O ho!" laughed they down the hall,
Knights and courtiers, one and all,
"Loves our Lady Bouverie."

"By my troth," cried he again,
"But my lord of Everden
Little recketh in his pride
What a rival eyes his bride.
Doughty warrior though he be,
He would tremble, sirs, pardie!
Could he see the youthful squire
That sits down before his fire."
"Ho, ho," laughed they in their glee,
"Rival claims in Bouverie!"

"Youthful squires have hearts of steel,"
Quoth the stripling lifting higher
His pure brow of lambent fire,
With a look of dauntless zeal.
"Not a noble in the land
Would do for the lady's hand,

What the simple youth you see
Would for her of Bouverie."

"Would you tilt a knightly lance
'Gainst yon chapel's broad expanse?
Mount the master's steed and clear
With one bound the narrow wier,
That you boast so loud and free?"
"I would die for her," said he;
"Tender maid of Bouverie!"

"Ho then, it were surely ill
One should balk you in your will;"
Sneering cried his fiery lord,
Raising high his mighty sword.
But the youth with smile of scorn,
And an aspect like the morn,
Met its sheen unflinchingly.
"You do show me grace," cried he,
"Haughty chief of Bouverie!"

"Is it so?" and in disdain
Fell that falchion once again.
"Then by Heaven that made us all,
Will we tip that grace with gall;"
And his gaze ran down the hall.
"Hugh of Elbert to the tower!
Rouse my daughter in her bower;
Tell her we would see her here
Ere yon eagle circling high
O'er our walls can disappear
In his realm of upper sky.
Woman's scorn has stinging point,
Pierces keenly through the joint;
We will see if he who eyes
All unmoved the falchion rise,
Can with equal spirit dare
The disdain of lady fair."

But the young man with a cry
Is already at his knee
Lifting hands impetuously.
"Baron Bouverie, let me die;
Slay me if thou wilt," he said;
"But O spare the tender maid,
Spare the maid of Bouverie."

"Do you fear her scorn so much?"
Cried the baron, while a smile
Or what men would fain call such,
Smote his iron lip the while.

"More than death," the young man said;
And a shadow dark and dread
Fell upon his youthful head.

"Do you think that she will be
All so harsh?" quoth Hugh of Dee
In the ear of Enderby.
"Frail as harebell swinging 'lone
On some turret's crumbling stone⬚
Do you think that he need fear
Such right bitter words to hear?"

But the baron's awful eye
Gloomed upon him for reply;
And as if a spell were hung
On each daring lip and tongue,
Silent grew both knight and lord,
Every eye with one accord
Fixed in close expectancy
On the face of Bouverie.

When, hark, hark, from where the door
Wavers restless o'er the floor,
Breaks a rustle and a stir
Like the breeze in mountain fir;
And there welleth into view
From the darkness dim and drear,
A fair face of light and dew,
And the noble maid is here.

O is this the haughty dame
Whose proud part it is to shame,
With her scorn, the stripling's love,
And his heart with anguish move?
This shy maiden, pale and sweet,
With the timid stepping feet,
And an eye like violets hid
Underneath each fearful lid?

Pausing in the narrow door,
Full within the view of all,
One slow smile she sends before
Her fair presence, down the hall.

Then as floats a cloud of snow
Into some fierce sunset's glow,
Through the crowd she softly sped,
And bent low her gentle head
'Gainst her haughty father's knee.
Fair and frail⬚ ah, who is he
Would cast shadow over thee,

Beauteous flower of Bouverie!

"Child of Bouverie, and heir
To the broad lands of Quermair;
Mistress of Dumont's fair bowers,
Gaverson and Heathcote's towers;
I have called you here to fling
Scorn upon a worthless thing."
Straight she looked up wondering.

If it be a worthless thing,
As you say, Lord Bouverie,
Little need is there to fling
Scorn upon it," murmured she.
"If I call you from your dreams
To set down my cup, it 'seems
You to do so," thundered he.

Like a summer snowdrop spurned
By a wind too strong for it,
Tremblingly her forehead turned
From that bitter-blowing wit.
"Let me know your will," she said,
And her lovely modest head
On her bosom faltered.

"It is this;" and heavily
On her arm his right hand fell;
"If you be of mine, 'tis well,
You will answer worthily.
Some one in this company
Hath dared boast his love for thee,
Heiress of proud Bouverie."
Flushed her cheek like red-rose tree.

"Not a lord⊡ " The long lash fell,
Fell like leaf across its flower
"Not a warrior⊡ " Ah, what spell
Holds the maiden in its power?
"Warrior-lord had met my sword,
But a woman's mocking word
Is the only answer meet
For a spurless squire, I weet."

For a spurless squire! oh
How her lips and forehead glow!
How the mounting rapture flies
From her chin unto her eyes!
Turning round with eager gaze,
On the youth she casts her eye,
And her smile is like a haze

Spreading o'er a roseate sky.

"By my soul!" the baron cries;
"But this scorn wears curious guise!"
And his teeth with iron grip
Close upon his nether lip.
O the sire is dread to see,
But a high tranquillity
Shrines the maid of Bouverie.

"Will you curse him, girl, or no?"
Shrieked the baron looming o'er her,
"Curse me, lady;" whispered low
He who knelt in homage 'fore her.
But the tender maiden stood
Trembling in the rushing flood
Whelming her sweet womanhood.

" 'Tis but shame," quoth Hugh of Dee,
"Let her pass, Lord Bouverie;
Not for stars is it I ween
To proclaim their state serene."
But the baron straight replied,
"Stars that tremble where they bide
Are not stars with which to crown
Ancient Bouverie's proud renown."

At which like some lily waking
From its moonlit dreams to find
Earth and air around it quaking
In a rage of gusty wind,
From her breast the maiden raised
To his face her glance amazed,
And her lips paled visibly.
Kneeling lowly at his knee,
"Ask me what you will," said she,
"Much would Claire of Bouverie do,
But this one thing, father, no."

"No!" and like a tiger stung
By the hunter's bitter dart,
From her side he backward sprung,
Eyes to heaven and hand to heart.

"What! and have I then come back
From the Paynim's fierce attack
To find treason in my home?
Saints of heaven! have I come
From the desert's wasting dearth,
From the raging of the sea,
From the tempest's enmity,

To find shame upon my hearth?"

"Shame? not so!" cried Hugh of Dee:
"Never shame," said Enderby;
"Love and patience, hope and truth,"
Spake in haste the gallant youth,
"But not shame, Lord Bouverie."
"Love and sorrow," whispered she;
"Only that, Lord Bouverie."

But as he might spurn a cur,
From his side he spurned her.
"Shame and worse than shame to me,
May the heavens right instantly
Smite thee, curse of Bouverie!"
Then while horror falls on all
In that dismal crowded hall.
Loud he clanked his ringing spur
With an awful look at her,
Through the dizzy moment's blur.
"Take her hence!" he loudly cried,
"Everden has lost his bride;
Fit for nought but death,⬜ her shame
Ne'er shall soil a warrior's name.
Take her hence; no more to me
Than this broken sword is she,
Henceforth here in Bouverie."
And his mighty blade he drew,
Brake it on his knee in two,
Cast it from him down the hall,
Lifted voice above them all,
"No more than that sword to me,
As I am Lord Bouverie!"

But at that an awful joy
Flushed the forehead of the boy;
"What the master flings aside,
One may surely have," he cried;
And with just a single bound,
Plucked the falchion from the ground.
"What the father gives to shame,
Love may freely, fully claim;"
And in sight of each man there
To his breast he drew her fair,
Wild, wan face with passionate care.

But the baron leaping back,
Struck that yearning twain apart,
As the lightning in its track
Open smites the sunset's heart.
"Do you claim her so, pardie?

By my life but we will see,
Daring cur of Bouverie,
Flowers like these though warped and dead,
Are not weeds," he fiercely said.
"If you think to pluck from me
This same rose of Bouverie,
By my life and by my wit
You will have to climb for it."
And he raised his hand on high,
Pointed through the casement nigh
To his turrets 'gainst the sky.

"In the top of yonder tower
Lies my lady daughter's bower;
If you love her as you say,
Mount and pluck her thence away.
Scarce so high as stars may be,
It will do, I wot," quoth he,
And his smile gloomed fearfully.

Mount the tower! from each man's tongue
One fierce cry of horror sprung.
Mount the tower, why it is death
And the maiden's startled breath
On her pale lip faltereth.
But the young man looming higher
Eyes his lord with glance of fire.

"Will you give her me to wife
If I win that steep with life?"
"Freely as yon heaven yields
Rain and sunshine to the fields."
"Then as Heaven loveth truth,
Cometh joy or cometh ruth,
Will I dare it!" cried the youth.

O will heaven look upon
Such a deed beneath the sun!
Ninety awful feet the steep
Towers above the donjon keep;
Ninety feet of rugged stone,
Crumbling, old, and ivy-grown▢
And each foot from top to pave,
A relentless, yawning grave!

But the young man at its base,
Sees no more that steep surface,
Sees no more the eager death
Biding him with hungry breath;
For upon the turret's height
They have placed the lady bright,

And his gaze is fixed upon
That dear head against the sun,
Whither all his hopes have run.

"O Lord Bouverie, swear to me,
If I win her thus from thee,
She shall be mine own for aye,
Wife and mistress from this day."
If you win her thus from me,"
Answered he of Bouverie,
"By my life but she shall be
Thine unto the judgment day."
"Then may Heaven be my aid,
And the right prevail!" he said,
And he laid his hand in power
On the base of that rude tower.
Through the crowd an icy chill
Shot and passed, and all was still.

"If I fail, let no man ever
Say I flinched from the endeavor;"
And he drew his body's weight
Up beyond the massive gate.
"If I fail, let no man's lip
Dare to taunt her with the slip;"
And he mounted 'fore their eyes
Unto where the turrets rise.
"If I fail⯑ " but at that word
Her sweet voice above was heard,
And he brake his speech in two;⯑
"But I will not fail, look you."

And with deathless zeal he bent
Will and strength to the ascent,
Setting now a steady foot
On the ivys' clinging root,
Grasping now the slippery edge
Of some narrow casement's ledge,
Arm upstretched and head backthrown,
As if her dear eyes alone
Drew him up those heights of stone.

O ye Heavens, what abyss!
If his daring hand should miss!
If the ivy's treacherous root
Should give way beneath his foot!
Many a gleam of horror flies
Through that watching maiden's eyes;
Many a noble heart below
Shudders in an awful woe⯑
If that daring hand should miss,

Saints of Heaven, what abyss!

But he mounts up yet for all
Past the gap within the wall,
Past the barbican's high crest,
Past the swallow's hidden nest;
Up, till heart and watching eye
Faint and follow wearily,
Till the swallows swooping whirl
Round and round in dizzy swirl,
And the clouds swim dreamily.

Slower now, but steady still,—
How the vines about him thrill!
Up another foot, and lo!
How his form sways to and fro!
Up one more, and he whose breast
Touch of gentleness doth know,
Drops his eyelids from the rest.

Further still, and lord and knight
Sink to ground in wild affright;
Only he of iron will,
Baron Bouverie, dares look still,
Dares to mark that figure high,
Swinging between earth and sky,
Past their help and past recall,
Eighty feet above them all.

He has gained the turret's brow,
Just beneath the lady now,
And his yearning arms reach high,
And her yearning arms reach low,
But their two hands— ah, so nigh,
Cannot join. "Ah ha!" then cries
The fierce lord, without disguise,
"In another moment more
This same silly sport is o'er!"
And he trims his iron lip
For the chill and awful smile
That shall hail the fatal slip
From that huge terrific pile.
But a sudden curse instead
Forces way betwixt his teeth,
For the maiden overhead
Leaning to the youth beneath,
Hath let down her scarf's deep fold,
And by its same help, behold,
He has struggled upward now
Level to the turret's brow.

"O Lord Bouverie, swear to me
That he lives," cried Hugh of Dee.
"Fifty candles, large and white,
To our Lady's shrine to-night,
If he wins the turrets height!"
Clamored noble Enderby.

But the baron with his eyes
Stretched and fixed upon the skies,
Answers not by deed or word
Anxious knight or fearful lord.
All his gaze is on the man
Struggling, fainting in the span
Of his lady's arms, upon
That last awful verge of stone,
Will he clear it? dare he?
Can It indeed be done by man?
Ha, he slips, he falls; but no
It was but the final throw
Of his body ere he put
O'er the ledge his fainting foot,

"'Tis no squire of mine," then cried
The fierce master in his pride,
"But some imp from hell we see
This same day in Bouverie."
But another moment, and
With a twist of foot and hand,
The brave stripling clears the edge
Of the turret's battled ledge,
And they see him leaning warm
On his lovely lady's arm,
Blessed at last and safe from harm.

O was ever such emprise
Seen before by mortal eyes!
Like the rising of the sea
Sprang the shout of victory;
Like the rising of the sea
When the heart of nature breaks,
Or the thunder when it speaks.

But the baron with a bound,
Jump'd in anger from the ground,
And his glance flashed fiercely round.
"Ah, but ye do well to shout
Ere the sport is full played out!
He has mounted up, I own,
And a gallant deed 'tis too,
But, my lords, remember yon,
That he has not yet come down!"

"Noble sir, what would you do?"
Cried out Vaux and Hamori too,
Leaping swiftly into view.
But the baron smiting-hard
With his feet upon the sward,
Cried, "As he has gone, I swear
He shall come again, or ne'er
Set his foot again to ground
From yon turret's narrow bound."

But at that brave Clarimaux,
Seizing hold of mighty Vaux,
Sprang before him in the way.
"Baron Bouverie," he said,
"You must o'er my body tread,
If you close that door to-day."
"Yes and mine!" re-echoed wide,
And stern Duffield leaped beside;
"We can look on gallant deeds,
Noble contests, lordly meeds,
But by Heaven that base heart bleeds
That would force these eyes to see
Grievous wrong and perjury."

"Do you think, then," cried his lord,
"That we bend to such as ye?
That because we lack our sword,
We will do your will?" shrieked he;
And with just one mighty bound
Cleft the swaying crowd around,
And stood breathing death before
The grim turret's narrow door,

When⯑ ah, what is this that meets
Him upon the threshold stone?
What this vision fair which greets
Him with tender arms outthrown?
Eye of fire and cheek of rose,
Lip where every rapture glows,⯑
Can this be the maiden frail
That but one short hour before
Lay like broken lily pale
On the castle's stony floor?
With a cry he backward sped,
But the maiden, springing, laid
On his breast her joyous head,
Smiling on him undismayed.
"Father, father, will you be
Harsher, then, than destiny?"
And her clinging, eager arm

Crept about him live and warm
With a wild and nameless charm.

But he like some rock that feels
All unmoved the wind's appeals,
For a moment stood unswayed,
Gazing down upon the maid.
But as closer to his breast
That pure cheek and forehead pressed,
Gentler aspects took the place
Of the frowns upon his face,
And a something like a sigh
Shook his bosom heavily.
Starting back with sudden speed,
From his neck her arms he freed,
And upon that crowd around
Fixed his haughty glance profound.
"Noble lords and sirs," he cried,
"We have looked this day upon
A great deed beneath the sun,
And our soul is satisfied.
But one thing remaineth yet
Which 'twere treason to forget;"
And he caught with fervor up
From the page beside, his cup:
" 'Tis the pledge which crowneth all
Gallant acts in field and hall."
Then while each man held his breath
In a doubt 'twixt life and death,
Back he tossed his head on high,
Raised the goblet towards the sky,
And spake out right potently:

"Here's to triumph in the wars!
Here's to pleasure in our halls!
Here's to Turkish scimitars
Hanging on our English walls!
Here's to courage, though it be
In a squire of low degree!
Here's to love! and here's to see,
Ere another day can flee,
These two wed in Bouverie!"

Premonition

The sweetest hour in all love's wondrous story,
When Hope first whispers of the coming glory.

A Sudden strange unfolding

In the cheerful noontide glare;
A sudden passionate heaving
In the bosom of the air.

The sense of something coming,
Mysterious and dread,
The lightning for its crowning,
The thunder for its tread.

A whisper in the breezes
One has not heard before;
A longing in the billow,
A yearning in the shore.

A bubbling up of life
From every wayside thing;
A meaning in the dip
Of even a swallow's wing.

A fear as if the morrow
Would ope some hidden portal;
A joy as if the feet
Stood at the gate immortal.

An angel in the pathway
To every common goal,
A widening of the outlook
That opens on the soul.

A sound of song at midnight,
A mist of dreams at noon;
A tear upon the eyelash,
The lips' smile might impugn.

A coming back of childhood
When morning suns are bright,
To find yourself a woman
Upon your knees at night.

In Light: In Night
Dark 'gainst the deepening skies,
Frosty with stars,
See I the bars
Of a weird cross arise.

How glooms the night away!
Winds are abroad;
Waves of the ford
Boom out a dismal lay.

Shrine wet with dew and tears

Here will I rest,
   Easing a breast
Worn by despair and fears.

Not on the brow of her
   Who walks in light,
   While I in night,
Let thy long shadow stir.

Rather across this heart
   Let it be laid,
   Shade after shade,
Gloom hath with her no part.

While in his sight her soul
   Greatens and glows,
   Till her heart's rose
Opes at his fond control;

I clasp the cross and cry
   "Strength, Holy Rood!"
   Kiss the cold wood
While at its foot I lie.

Angel, whose wings I see
   Shift 'mongst the stars,
   Make these chill bars
Ladders of light for me.

Three Letters

I

From Him To Her

Sweet, when I gave my troth to you
   I loved you—or imagined so;
But winds may change, and clouds that blew
   To Eastward at the morn, may blow
   Toward the West, by noon, you know.

'Tis not that you are grown less fair;
   A rose is e'er a rose to me;
But he who wanders on to where
   The pensive violet clusters are,
   May chance forget the rose, you see,

And I have wandered: there, 'tis out!
   However fickle, false, or wrong,

You cannot say I gave to doubt
    The master music of that song
    Joy sings in breasts where hopes belong.

You cannot say I was not true
    To truth, if not to constancy;
That I still sought to quaff the dew
    From off the rose, while secretly
    I groped for what more pleased me.

Nor will you, being sweet as fair,
    Condemn that other fair one's sweetness;
Nor by those charms which make so rare
    Your own pure face, disdain the meetness
    Of loving grace in its completeness.

For beauty, beauty is; and—well,
    A man must worship where he must;
Yet if you chose to hold me, Belle,
    Why, I am yours; I would be just;
    I pledged, and will fulfill my trust.

And if I wed I will be true;
    You need, not fear; the wave which holds
A lily up to all men's view,
    Scarce spots the silver of its folds
    With restless wash of secret molds.

Then tell me, sweet; is't yes or no—
    A marriage ring, or short farewell?
Do you still love me, or love so
    You can forgive?—The wedding bell
    'Gins ringing—then what say you? tell.

II

From Her To Him

What should I say but farewell; is the rose
    A thing too slight to stand alone and still
When the wind leaves it? Shall a flower that grows
    In God's clear light, more dearly love the thrill
Of its own petals, than the happy sound
    Of breezes singing, though their songs should be
        For some sweet other blossom far away,
    That is no rose to lose them? No; the bliss
        Of him to whom I gave my bliss one day
Is much more precious than his troth to me:
    I scarce would wish his face again to see,
    Its happy smile and tender shine to miss;

Then of the twain it is not yes, but no,
   And with the no, farewell. May she, your love,
So live in joy and so in beauty move,
     You never may in all your dreams forget
     Heaven blooms for you within the violet,

III

From Him To Her

Ah, rose, my rose, my love, my queen,
   My gentle, faithful, tender heart;
The one fair woman I have seen
   With soul to feel for other's smart;
Didst think that I who once had known
   Thy wild-rose touch could wander on?

That any blossom 'neath the sun,
   Though crowned with heavenly grace and power,
Could fairer seem to me than one
   Whose blushes are the summer's dower?
That daintiest violets in the world
   Could rival rose-buds half unfurled?

Didst think—but no, thou didst not think—
   Thou didst but love! O sweet! O wife!
My one firm hold upon the brink
   Of that deep gulf which we call life,
Would thou couldst know my joy to find
This angel living in thy mind.

For, sweet, I love thee, loved thee so;
   But oh! so feared to trust my love,
Who am no saint, and needs must know
   How false the fairest face can prove;
How oft beneath the softest sigh
Heaves woman's heart of vanity.

And soul yields not but to its own;
   And I did love thee with my soul;
A stream sings on by weed and stone,
   But ocean billows long to roll
The strength and glory of the seas,
Upon their shore of mysteries.

And thou wert shore and all to me;
   My star, my crown, my calm retreat;
So dear that I could bear to pain
   Thy heart to learn its secret sweet.

Canst pardon then? O sunny shore,
A whole sea waits to tell thee more.

Thou wilt not scorn me? Ah, my pen
    Slips at the wild thought to the floor;
Nought else but eyes can plead, love, whe
    The ghost of death stands in the door;
Then read what I have writ, and say
If love can pardon love alway,

Thou dost not speak. O sweet! O love!
It were not much to die for thee,
But live and know not God above
Could give my heaven back to me—
Ah, canst thou doom it? What, yes? no!
O God, mayst Thou but pardon so!

Pearls

The wave that floods the trembling shore,
    And desolates the strand,
In ebbing leaves, 'mid froth and wreck,
    A shell upon the sand.

So troubles oft o'erwhelm the soul;
    And shake the constant mind,
That in retreating leave a pearl
    Of memory behind.

Shadows

A zephyr moves the maple-trees,
    And straightway o'er the grass
The shadows of their branches shift,
    Shift, Love, but do not pass,

So though with time a change may come,
    Within my steadfast heart,
The shadow of thy form may stir,
    But cannot, Love, depart.

Paul Isham

I

When first Paul Isham crossed the fields to woo
Sweet Gladys Darrell in her humble home,
'Twas deemed the veriest marvel of the year
By all our country gossips. "True," said they,
"She has some beauty, is not quite devoid
Of grace in speech and bearing; is both young
And gentle tempered, but despite all this,
A match unworthy of his name and wealth,
His varied learning and a culture won
By years of foreign travel."

He it was
Who built the sumptuous mansion which you see
Rise in the vale below us. There in state
As lonely as methinks 'tis cheerful now,
He lived on his return from o'er the seas,
Respected, courted somewhat, but unmoved
By woman's smile from his accustomed mien
Of proud composure, till his glances fell
On pretty Gladys where she stood one day
Amid her fellows. As a wilding rose
Discovered in a garden draws the gaze
And seems in its meek loveliness more fair
Than all its prouder sisters, so to him
She seemed the choicest blossom of them all,
A treasure past computing. For a year
He wooed her, then, as doth the strong man woo
His last and dearest blessing from the fates,
And at the year's end won her. Then to him
Returned the morning freshness of his youth,
Hope and the joy of life. She was to him
A breath of spring across the winter rime,
And in her beauty he was wont to see
Something akin to all that sweetest is
In Nature's handiwork, when from the snow
The crocus blossoms, and the earth, beguiled,
Yields up her hoarded treasures to the sun
And all mankind rejoices.

But of late
He had perceived a certain change in her;
The bud which gazes fearless on the sky
Droops as its being richens; so with her
Across whose girlish merriment had crept
The hush of feeling and the calm of thought.
Less often rang the songs that once had seemed
Surcharged with laughter like the voice of brooks;
But if by chance they fell upon the ear
They lingered there, like waves which vainly seek
To utter all the story of the sea
And die in music with the tale untold.

Less frequent shone the smile upon her lips;
But when it came 'twas sweeter than before,
As the lone ray that wanders through a glen,
Suggesting beauties it but half reveals,
Is lovelier than the sunshine on the lea.
And when Paul Isham saw all this he said,
"The summer grows upon my darling's heart,
Ripening her woman's nature."

June was here,
And in a month 'twas thought the marriage peal
Would ring from Benton church-bells. In the house
Beyond the maples there was heard at times
Unwonted sounds, as though its generous lord
Was making preparation for his bride;
And every evening when the sun was low
And earth and air were radiant, he was seen
Crossing the meadow to his Gladys' home
Beneath the mountain. Oft he passed alone,
But oftener still in company with Ralph,
A youthful brother, who had haply come
Some two months since from his far home in town,
To stray again among remembered scenes,
And with man's eyes behold the sacred spots
Where in his dreamy childhood he had stood
And seen the visions of his future life
Flit by in sun and shadow.

But this eve
It pleased Paul Isham to go forth alone
To meet with Gladys, For all through the day
The thought of her had called a rainbow forth
From every cloud of care, and much he yearned
For her dear presence. O the toils of life!
How small they seem when love's resistless tide
Sweeps brightly o'er them! Like the scattered stones
Within a mountain streamlet, they but serve
To strike the hidden music from its flow
And make its sparkle visible.

A copse
Full of soft shadows and sun-lighted glades
Lay in his path. Here he was wont to pause
And cull some woodland blossom from the mould
To lay within her palm, that it might speak
Such words as he in his heart-reverence found
Halt in the utterance. But to-night his thoughts
Sprang wingèd to his lips; his very love
Seemed given for inspiration, and he trod
Hastily onward, feeling in his soul
A yearning like the yearning of a wave

That sees the shore stretch beautiful beyond it.
He found her pacing o'er the sunlit lawn,
Lost in a dream that brought the fitful blood
In tremor to her cheek, and lent withal
To her high bearing such a tender grace—
No moonbeam sleeping in a chancels dusk,
Amid the splendor of emblazoned gules,
Could be more fair, or sweetlier blend in one
The light of heaven and the glow of earth.

"Gladys," he said, and smiling drew her hand
Closely in his; "my heart is full to-night,
Full of true love for you, dear, as mine eyes
Are full of your rare beauty. Scarce can I
In my great happiness and glad content,
Believe that I have known you but a year,
Who now are joy, love, hope, and heaven to me,
That once knew none of these. For I have had
Through all my years a lonesome life and dark,
With overmuch of sorrow, and I stand
Just now where yonder hills stood at the dawn,
'Twixt night and sunshine: in the future thee,
But in the past a long array of griefs,
Crushed hopes, ambitions lost, sweet friendship made
A mockery and a snare—a life of woe
Without a love to comfort.

"I've a fancy,
A strange wild fancy, that we two were friends
Long, long ago, in an existence past,
And now but half remembered. In your face
I found no strangeness when I first beheld you,
Only the blossoming of some vague dream
Into sweet life and glad reality.
I do remember how in vain that day
I sought for that which had suggested you
And made your glance familiar; how my thoughts
Flew back in wavering flight along the years,
E'en to the smile upon my mother's lips,
When in her arms I lay, a little child
Unconscious of my bliss, and felt my thoughts
Float on the music of her voice until
They stranded on the flowery shores of sleep.
But though her loveliness was like a breath
Of sunset glory on a silver cloud,
It was not yours."

"You lost your mother, Paul!"
"Yes, Gladys, and with her the roseate hues
Which make the morn of childhood beautiful.
Thereafter life took sterner shades and thrilled

But to one touch, Ambition's. 'I will be
Great!' was my watchword for the day;
And when at eve I laid my head to rest,
'Twas still, 'I will be great!' And so I toiled,
Struggled and anguished for a space of years
Along the rugged steeps which lead to Fame,
Feeling the need of love wax strong within
As my ways thickened. Why, in those hard days
The least child's smile would stir me to the heart
Like far off music, and a gentle word
Uttered in merest welcome or farewell,
Had power to soothe me like a breeze which brings
The south up on its pinions. Marvel not
That such slight things had power to move me; know
That he who steps on stones is glad to feel
The smallest spray of moss beneath his feet.

"But, Gladys, I was pressing with the crowd
And with the crowd I faltered. Not for me
To jostle bruised and bruising to the goal
Where, on the rocky pinnacles of Fame,
Cluster the living garlands. So that hope
Died also, and I buried it and stood
Awhile above its grave, then went my way
Still without love or comfort."

Ceasing there,
He gazed a moment on her half-turned cheek
And lowered lashes, marveling at the tears
Within her eyes, but finding her withal
More lovely to behold than when the rose
Lived in perpetual summer on her cheek.
For beauty such as hers is like a breath
Of distant music stealing through the hush
Of fragrant gardens, and like music draws
It's rarest charm from gentle melancholy.
But even a pearl will flush with sudden lights
If but the sun fall on it; so the cheek
Which but a moment since was pale as snow,
Grew dazzling with its shifting play of flame
Ev'n as he gazed upon it, and the lips
Which had been very silent, woke and said.
And was there not one, then, of all your friends,
Whose frank affection could redeem the loss
Of these sad years? Though joy and hope were gone.
You had a brother, Paul."

"True, Gladys, true;
But we were bred in separate homes, and he
Has ever lived 'neath happier skies than I,
And known less sorrow. Born for joy alone.

He thrids the world as sunshine thrids a wood.
And all men love him, as in weal or woe
They never yet have loved or cherished me.
But child, you weep! Ah, have I then with words
Moved you so deeply, Gladys? Know you not
That such a joy as lives within me now.
Can, like the strings of an Æolian harp.
Draw music from the roughest wind that blows
From those past hours of sorrow? Weep no more.
Or weep for joy alone."

"Alas!" she cried,
"The eye that pierces straightly to the future
Can never weep for joy."

"The future, Gladys?"

"Yes," and a sad smile flickered through her tears
Like a faint rainbow from a summer shower,
Which ere it arches 'gins to fade away.
"Yon sky blooms very rosily," she said,
"But look you where the shadowy palm of night
Steals up to pluck its roses. Hark," she cried,
"Hear how the brooks below us in the woods
Twang on the stones! Like strings of silver bells
They laugh and sport as if all time were theirs,
Whereas already by their careless waves
The hot-mouthed Summer stoops her down to drink
The draught that is their death. Oh!" she said,
"Full many a vessel threads the gates of morn,
With spreading sails and gold upon its prow,
That ere the eve will bend beneath the storm.
And we—how know we if our moments run
To break on joy or sorrow? We can hope,
But hope itself is born of doubt, my friend,
Always in bud, but never quite a flower."

"True, Gladys; but the trouble in your eyes
Hath borrowed darkness from a surer fear
Than this vague terror of an unknown morrow.
Then trust me with it, let me bear it for you;
Have I not vowed within mine inmost soul
To hold you much more precious than the world,
Yes, as the very blood within my veins,
And will you not then trust me?"

"Trust you?" she cried,
"Would unto God," she whispered, "would to God
All things came easy as my trust in you,"
"Then speak, I do constrain you; by your love
I do constrain you, Gladys. Silent yet?

Nay then," he said, and smiling, laid his hands
With tender care on either troubled cheek,
"I'll read your sorrows where I've read your joys,
 Ev'n in your eyes, beloved."

But she, like one
Struck to the heart by some quick shame or grief,
Shrank trembling back, nor met his gaze with hers,
But bowed her head and prayed him to forbear,
Saying that on the morrow; if he willed,
She would disclose him all her secret care,
But that for this one day she must crave patience.

But ah, when morrow came and he returned
To that same spot beneath the woodland trees,
It was to find not Gladys, but a letter
Lying upon their simple rustic seat,
In which with many cries for his forgiveness,
She told him all her heart. How for long weeks
The truth had grown upon her as a cloud
Grows o'er the sun, that not as he loved her
Could she love him. That liking and respect
Were not what he desired, nor what she
Had hoped alone to give him when she pledged
Hand unto hand and willing heart to heart,
And yet that these were all she truly had
To give for so great love as he gave her.
And how this knowledge had o'ershadowed her,
Filling her nights with anguish and her days
With heavy shame and struggle, till her life
Grew bitter to her, and his words like swords
Cleft her and left deep wounds that would not heal.
And how in honor to his noble faith
She could no more deceive him, though her heart,
Her woman's fearful, trembling heart should break
With anguish for his sorrow. "Oh!" she wrote,
"Far liever had I died in my first youth,
Than lived to be a heavy grief to one
So noble and so loving. Blame me not;
For I have wrestled with my heart as one
Wrestles with fate itself; and all in vain."

It was a deadly blow! A blow like that
Which swooping unawares from out the night
Dashes a man from some high starlit peak
Into a void of cold and hurrying waves.
'Twas not the loss alone. In that wild hour
Of first resistance, anguish, and despair,
He felt he could have borne her simple loss
So God had taken her. But loss of love!
Loss of belief in all the radiant past,

Of hope in years to come—ah, who but those
Whose lives have felt the shock of utter wreck,
Can rightly speak of what that hour of doom
Was to this man of sorrow!

Or when later,
She with her sweet face worn by bitter tears,
Her young form trembling and her hands outstretched,
Came stealing through the forest to his side,
And kneeling at his feet entreated him
To look on her with pity and not blame,
For she had never meant to do him wrong,
What tongue can tell the feelings of his heart
As taking that bright head between his hands
He looked upon her face and gently said,
"Indeed, indeed, I do not blame you, Gladys,
God knows I love you with too deep a love
To seek to rob you for my selfish ends
Of that dear right which gives to woman's vow
Its heart significance. Nor would I seek
By any plea of loss in hope or love
To make your loss the greater. But, dear child,
There yet is left to manhood one true plea,
The plea of your own happiness. For child,
I know That I can make you happy. There is that
Hid in this breast which needs must call from yours
Some echo in the years that are to come.
And Gladys, Gladys, though you know it not,
No other man can give what I have given,
Nor were it well he should. It is your youth
Which has been speaking. Youth has needs, I know,
And headlong yearnings like the mountain streams
That rush adown the nearest path they find
To meet the sounding river; but, oh child,
In womanhood the heart is like the sea,
Deep, deep, and self-contained, but yearning still
Through all its mighty billows for a shore
To break in strength upon. Remember this;
And by the stately womanhood I see
Budding within the gentle girl I love,
Pause ere it be too late." And with the gleam
Of something like a smile upon his lips,
He held his hand out, whispering in her ear,
"If be you cannot answer me for tears,
But lay your hand, though e'er so light, on mine,
And I shall understand."

But she as though
Made frantic by her helplessness and grief,
Struck her two palms together as in prayer,
And stood there murmuring with white lips,

"O Christ,
Help me! Thou who renouncedst thy will and life,
Hear me this hour!"

Then unto him there came
An awful change, and from her side he turned
Away and hunted slowly for the sun
Like one whom God has blinded. "Child," said he,
"You have not told me all,"

"No, no," she cried,
"I have not told you all." And bowing down
As though she fain had knelt before his face,
She whispered of another love than his
Which had, though all unconscious, caught her heart
Within its subtle radiance. "Oh!" she said,
"I meant to be most true; but when he came,
And when he spake and looked on me and smiled,
I know not how but all my life seemed changed.
And yet he came, and I for very shame
Could not forbid his coming. How could I,
Since you were blind, and he had said no words
Save as friends speak or brothers! Bear with me;
I am most weak, but for your sake will strive,
Yes, and will conquer, so you send him hence
Where we may meet him never."

"Send him hence?
I send him hence? As friends speak or as brothers?
You tremble so I cannot understand—
As brothers, Gladys, brothers?" And she saw
A stony pallor steal across his face.
And felt his hand fall heavy on his breast
As he had had a blow too dread for words.

"Ah, my false heart, what hast thou done?" she moaned,
And drawing nearer, touched his sleeve and strove
To look upon his face; and called him Paul,
Dear Paul, and laid her head against his arm
Sobbing, "I am to be your wife; O Paul,
Hear me, your wife!" But he, in nowise moved,
Answered her not save with a single word
That fell as hopes fall, or as if all life
Went with it, and that word was Ralph.

She heard
And thrilled through all her being like a harp
Touched in the passing; while across her lip
A light passed and upon her tearful cheek
Rested, as though the very name had power
To rouse her beauty, as a tremulous wind

Opens unto its depths a wild-wood flower.
But he who bent above her shivered once
Through all his frame, and, glancing down, unloosed
Her hands from off his arm and turned away
Blindly toward the shadows. Then once more
Did Gladys in an ecstasy of pain
Entreat him for a word, a look, a sign
Of his forgiveness; striving hard to break
The spell which bound him, holding out her hands
And telling o'er her simple tale again
With many words of sorrow and remorse
And hard self-accusation; till at last
He turned and looked upon her with a sigh
And said, "Poor child!" and still as in a dream,
Once more, "Poor child!" and so passed by and moved
Heavily away into the shadowy dusk.
And lo! as thus he went, far in the West
The last faint crimson died, while chill and keen
A wind came winging through the gates of night
And o'er the valley blew, until the trees
Bowed down their heads and all was dark and drear,
Where but an hour ago was bloom and joy,
Sunshine and color and the song of birds.

It was the end; or e'er three days had passed,
This letter, breathing love's renunciation,
Was placed in Gladys' hand; "Dear child;
You will forgive me that I do not come
To say farewell, since farewell must be said;
You will forgive me, Gladys, It is meet
That I should go. I love you, dear, too much

To wed you. 'Twere not well, not well indeed,
That I who feel the pressure of my years
Heavily at times, should mate with one so young
The violets are blowing in her life.
Then take this boon from me and hold it choice,
As I have held it while I called it mine,
Take back yourself, dear; not in grief but peace,
For I am blessèd only in your joy,
Nor fear to yield your maiden troth again,
For he is very noble and will hold
You precious, else I had not left you, Gladys.
And he will make you happier far than I,
As he is happier-natured. Trust in him,
And his glad spirit like a golden bell
Will answer to the lightest touch of thine,
Filling your home with melody. And now
No less I bless you that I write this day
Against my name the tender title
Brother."

But Gladys, in whose gentle bosom glowed
The light of purest purpose, felt her soul
Recoil before this prospect of delight
Built on another's woe. "What, go my ways
Girded with happiness and gay with hope,
While he whose hand hath clung to mine in troth,
Walks in the shadow cast by my delight,
An exile from his home! No, no, O no!
If hearts are weak, souls should at least be strong;
I cannot as true woman do this thing."

And though with added thought and certain proof
That he had gone to come again no more,
Rose many shy sweet pictures of the bliss
Which might be hers would she but turn to meet
The passion glowing in young Isham's eyes,
She gave it as her final verdict out,
That while his brother lived she ne'er should give
Her hand unto another, troth at least,
If not her heart, being her own to grant
Or to withhold as faith and duty prompted.
Nor though she was of gentlest mind and heart
Could she be moved from this by any plea
Wisdom or love could urge, but firm and true
Kept to her faith, though day by day her cheek
Paled, and the glance so proudly radiant once
Grew all so dim, that those who held her dear
Shrank as they looked upon her wan young face,
Crying within their hearts, "The child will die."

And they were right; had there not come a change
Fair Gladys would have died. 'Twas not that love
Had built so firm a seat within her spirit,
That disappointment threatened all with ruin,
But that the seeds of wild remorse were there,
A grievous sense of wrong to those two hearts
So firm and generous in their deep devotion.
But ev'n as life seemed bending 'neath its load,
There came to Benton tidings of the wreck,
With loss of all on board, of the good ship
In which Paul Isham voyaged to the East.
And keen as was the pang of grief his death
Brought to her faithful soul, the strain that bore
So hard upon her tender soul was eased;
And like a flower that shakes the first light snow
From its transparent leaves, she thrilled anew
To life and to a beauty more replete

For the faint hint of sorrow in its joy.

But though young Ralph came wooing with the spring,
Fair Gladys would not listen till the year
Of widowhood and mourning was fulfilled.
"For I was his betrothed," she whispered low,
"And being such, should feel my shame complete,
If I should wind a wreath around my brow
Ere a year's stars could circle o'er his grave."
But when the early Fall had surely brought
All spring hopes to fulfillment, these were wed,
And in the glow of their perfected love
Found happiness at last and full content
Beyond their fondest dreaming. Yet withal
There was a wave of sorrow in the joy
Of Gladys' breast at least; a gentle wave
That yet made saddest music, when it throbbed
Across the hush of midnight or the swell
Of careless mirth in which she took no part.

For now it was she 'gan to dream strange dreams
Of him whom they deemed perished, but whom she
Saw ever moving free amongst his kind,
A living, breathing man. So plain indeed
She saw this noble figure come and go
Amid the lighter fancies of her sleep,
She scarce could tell or that were life or this
First waking with the sun upon her cheek
And he no longer near. And still so oft
This single dream returned, she seemed to live
A double life beneath the skies, and give
One half to him she loved, and one to him
Who loving her had perished for her sake.
Yet not as though she met him face to face,
She saw him, dreaming; but as one who moved
Before her in a life which was not hers,
And yet was life with earnest hopes and cares
And duties manifold. And now as one
Who bends above the couches of the sick,
She saw him from afar, a steady light
Among a whirl of shadows; now as one
Who striveth with a heaving, threatening crowd
That beat about him restlessly and wild,
While he stands firm, a tower of stately strength,
Amid a sea of waves; and now again
Alone and musing o'er an empty hearth,
With just a tress of gold within his hand—
She knows, ah, who so well! But whether thus,
Or whether moving in the hurrying crowd
Of street or church or mart, forever calm,
Forever with that smile upon his lips

Which spake of sorrow past and peace regained.
So deep this smile, so deep the faithful gaze
That sometimes turned upon her from afar,
Demanding not but blessing, that she woke
Ofttimes in tears, to find her arms stretched out
Across her husband to the silent stars,
And waking, shudders, that a dream should be
More vital true than life. And though at first
She fain had told her husband all her heart
And all her grief and yearning, yet as time
Rolled slowly by and brought her no relief,
She learned to hush her secret in her breast,
And ponder it in silence when the stars
Clomb slowly past the turrets of the house,
And lingered in the swaying trees beneath,
Like troops of steady watchers.

Thus the years
Passed slowly by, but not until there lay
A second blooming infant on her knee,
Did she dare whisper to her soul and say,
Her friend Paul Isham lived. But even then
She spake not, seeing men so rarely trust
To woman's intuitions, but would sit
Ofttimes and muse, her chin within her palm,
Like one who looks on visions from afar,
No other eye can see.

And now there came
A certain day when Gladys felt her doubts
Grow to a sure belief within her breast,
No after-thought might shake. She had been sitting
Beside an open casement where the vines
Slow creeping from below but half concealed
The rounded beauty of her cradling arms
And tender mother-smile. Across the hush
Of the calm twilight she could hear the voice
Of little Paul, as o'er the lawn beneath
He fluttered half in view, when suddenly
There came a silence so assured and deep,
She felt as though a sudden gate had oped
Deep in her soul, through which a bursting light
Swift pouring, checked the breath upon her lips
In sacred wonder. Rising swiftly up,
She laid the sleeping infant from her arms,
And stood in all her loveliness revealed,
The light of feeling shimmering on her face
Like summer starlight on a trembling wave.
And lo! as thus she stood, there came a sound,
A whispered sigh, a sudden stifled moan,
That even as she listened passed away.

But when a little later she beheld
A muffled form emerge from out the trees
And vanish in the shadows of the lawn,
She felt a sudden fever smite her soul,
And bounding forward, let one single cry
Leap towards it through the vines, then tottering, sank
All helpless with her hands across the sill,
But with her face still turned the way he went,
As if her look alone might serve in power
To bring him back again.

And thus it was
Her young son found her when he came in haste
To tell her of a stranger he had met
But now among the trees. "So bowed," he cried,
"I scarce could see his face, and yet so strong
He took me in his arms and kissed me, mother,
As I have seen you kiss the little cross
That was the gift of my dear uncle Paul."

And she who listened bent her head once more,
And through the sacred tremor of her tears
Cried softly, "Yes, my son, strong, strong indeed;
The earth holds no such other." Then in haste
Uprising, caused an instant hurried search
For one, a stranger, passed but now from view
Across the twilight grounds. But though they sought
From early evening till the stars were bright,
They found him not, and when the morrow came
'Twas told her how the stranger seen last eve
Had passed away at midnight from the town,
To come again no more. And pondering this,
She felt the shadows lift from off the past,
And show her, as in some strange magic glass,
The story of the years, and how his heart
Had loved her so, he rather chose the ways
Of lonely exile than to cry as false
The dire report which, like an open gate
Had wooed her feet into the paths of joy.
And moved to the pure depths of her true heart,
She bowed her head and vowed, with God's high aid,
To make her life a blessing and a prayer,
That in the pure and freer world to come,
She might stand unrebuked by conscious wrong,
Betwixt the noble twain whose love had been
The grief and solace of her earthly years,
And looking up in either shining face,
See benediction there. And though from this
Her dreams forsook her to return no more,
There used to steal at times across her ear
A sound, a whisper, like a wave that broke

Far on a lonely shore: "Grieve not for me,
For I am blessed only in your joy,
So for my sake be happy."

Rosa, Dying

Then this is death—
How strange, how strange! Another hour,
Another breath Of joyous life, of love, and all is o'er,
The scarcely opened blossom perished in its flower!

And I so young!
Ah, when I first awoke to hear
The music rung
From what had once been only held so dear,
Because in outward show it glimmered bright and clear;

(As children prize
The shell whose pearl is breathed o'er
With vermeil dyes,
Yet feel their joy grow deeper than before
When taught by loving care the secret of its roar;)

It seemed to me
The longest life was all too fleet
An ecstasy,
For one to hear the mighty ages beat
Their hidden meanings out in harmony complete.

And now I die!
And all the hopes which girlhood hath,
Go softly by,
Stranding upon the silent shores of Death;
Like little boats blown home by twilight's purple breath.

Nay rather, Heart,
Like little boats that at the dawn
In joy depart,
And on towards the open sea are borne,
Where rounds to perfect noon, a vague, imperfect morn.

One Month

A little month ago, and in my ear
I heard your low "I love" strike warm and clear,
And musing, wondered why with that pure word
Held to my bosom like a fluttering bird,

I yet could pace the budding earth and find
No gladder angel singing in the wind.
To-night with ear turned vainly to the breeze,
Which brings no sound save that of moaning trees,
With lips unwarmed by thy pure kiss, and hands
Held out unclasped across the severing lands,
I sit and muse, and musing seem to hear
A seraph's voice in every quiring sphere.
A month ago, and Love and May in vain
Looked in my face and sang their sweetest strain,
This chill June eve with none to smile and say,
"Sweet, how I love thee!" bears the palm away.
Why, why is this? Can Summer cheat us so
Of heart and soul? Ah, dear, dost thou not know?
May's laughing eyes beheld thy love for me,
But June looks down upon my love for thee.

At The Piano

Play on! Play on! As softly glides
   The low refrain, I seem, I seem
To float, to float on golden tides,
   By sunlit isles, where life and dream
Are one, are one; and hope and bliss
Move hand in hand, and thrilling, kiss
      'Neath bowery blooms,
       In twilight glooms,
And love is life, and life is love.

Play on! Play on! As higher rise
   The lifted strains, I seem, I seem
To mount, to mount through roseate skies,
   Through drifted cloud and golden gleam,
To realms, to realms of thought and fire,
Where angels walk and souls aspire,
And sorrow comes but as the night
That brings a star for our delight.

Play on! Play on! The spirit fails,
The star grows dim, the glory pales,
The depths are roused—the depths, and oh!
The heart that wakes, the hopes that glow!
The depths are roused: their billows call
The soul from heights to slip and fall;
To slip and fall and faint and be
Made part of their immensity;
To slip from Heaven; to fall and find
In love the only perfect mind;
To slip and fall and faint and be

Lost, drowned within this melody,
As life is lost and thought in thee.

Ah, sweet, art thou the star, the star
That draws my soul afar, afar?
Thy voice the silvery tide on which
I float to islands rare and rich?
Thy love the ocean, deep and strong,
In which my hopes and being long
To sink and faint and fail away?
I cannot know. I cannot say.
    But play, play on.

In Farewell

I met thee, dear, and loved thee—yet we part,
Thou on thine unknown way and I on mine,
Ere yet the music of my woman's heart
  Has had full time to harmonize with thine.
Yet since the strain begun has seemed so sweet,
  Forgive me if I dare to proffer thee
This echo from the depths where all complete
  Trembles the soul's perfected melody.
  Jewels I have not, else for memory
Would I bestow them on the friend I love,
But tears and smiles, and the sweet thoughts that move
The heart by day and night, such, such to thee
I give in these poor lines as lavishly
As summer winds yield fragrance when they blow
Up from a vale where countless roses grow.

A Tragedy of Sedan

I had seen him in battle, and he was a man
To watch in a conflict—had seen him when death
Struck down at his feet the one comrade he loved—
But never before, upon field or in camp,
Had beheld on his face such a look of the grave,
As he brought yesternight to the door of my tent
When the evening guns sounded. So ghastly it was,
So dread in suggestion of anguish, I leapt
In dismay to my feet. Was he ill? Was he hurt?
But his eyes staring on without sight made me pause.
'Twas not death, but despair; and I hastily cried,
"The man has lost hope, is in grief—"

But at that

He was straight at my side with a bound: "Ay, in grief!
And you talk of it, you! talk of grief! but 'tis easy.
We all talk of grief. I have heard of a man
Who looked at a scaffold above him and said—
Laughjng too as he spake—'If by chance it should fall,
'Twould crush me, no doubt.' When a moment from that
It did fall, he shrieked. Ah, yes—" he went on,
"Was it strange? Just as I could shriek now who behold—
But enough. I must tell you the whole from the first,
Or go mad before morning. My friend—" and his eyes
Glared wildly on mine through his thick, fallen hair—
"Have you loved? Yes," he went on more shrill, "in the pause
Of the death-dealing guns one may ask—may he not?—
Such a question as that of a man."

For reply
I drew from my bosom a curl that I kissed,
And put back on my heart without word. 'Twas enough.
He bent down at my side with a cry: "Is she fair?
Hath she eyes like a dove and a step like a deer,
So gentle and wild? Do you love her—O Heaven!—
With the force of your body, your spirit, and heart?
With a flame and a star in your soul? Ah!" he gasped,
"It is folly to ask: a woman must die
Or turn false to be loved so. Pray God—" and he paused
With a sudden quick clench of his hand—"you may die
Ere you come to a passion like that."

Looking down,
He took from his finger a ring which he wore,
Gazed on it a moment in anguish, then said:
"She was pledged to me, friend; was my hope from a child;
Was my life, you might say. In the mesh of her glance
All my being was thralled. Not a dawn rose upon me
But I woke with the thought of her beauty. The sun
Was not more to mine eyes than her smile. Ah, I know
Such a love is not good—that its passion undoes
What its purity makes. But a man cannot choose
His fate from the heavens; and this love, as it was,
Was my fate.

"Well, her heart gave response to my suit,
And we had been wedded two long years ago;
But love is ambitious. To give her a home
I left her, and far from her glance and her smile,
Worked my way up to fortune. Oh, oh, the long months!
But they passed, and at length, like a dawn on the night,
Came the day of return. Ah, that day! Like a flame
It flares ever before me; her looks and her smiles
Will not flit, will not fly. As we walked up the street
The bells brake out ringing. For three months of doom

I have heard them; they never have ceased in my ears
Day and night, night and day. But, strange as it seems,
At the moment they rang, I was deaf. 'Twas her voice
Whose music I listened to then. In her hand
She bore a white lily; and when at the fount
The children came down from the village to crown
Her locks with wild posies plucked up from the woods,
I scarcely do think I had heard yonder guns
Had they split at my side. Do you marvel, then, friend,
I was deaf to his voice, though he stood at her sleeve
Like a brother?

"But no dwelling on that. 'Tis enough
I was happy that day; that its glory was like
The flushing of sunset across the wild waste
Of a billowy sea ere the night fell. Ah! ah!
You wonder what now!
You, sitting at ease, in your tent, with the tress
Of a tender, true woman like balm on your breast,
Wonder what could have turned all this rapture to woe
In a moment Ah, God! 'twas not much! Just a rent
In the woof of my fair nuptial garment! Not much;
Only this; When I rose in the dusk from my guests
('Twas my wedding-eve, friend; she had smiled on me, too,
But an instant before) my beloved was gone!
Yes, yes," he shrieked out, "gone as certain as joy—
Gone, gone, gone, gone! Not a word of farewell,
Not a look: just that smile that was love, or like love,
And then this great gulf.

"Oh, oh may the world
Grow old and shrink up in the hands of the Lord
Ere another night creep by like that!
Not till morn Did they tell me the whole—how for weeks he had been
In the town at her side; stealing up in the dusk
To drop a stray rose in her hand—how for weeks
She had drooped her sweet head and said never a word
When the neighbors would ply her with questions.
I say
It was not until morning they told me all this,
Meantime she was gone.

"Well, I lived—lived to seek him.
Do you know what that means? By the chances of war
You have been in your time the hunted, spent deer;
Have you e'er been the hound? Can you reckon of days
When, with fire in your blood and revolt in your brain,
You wandered the world with your eyes on the face
Of each man that you met? And the nights—
The nights without sleep; and the dreams—
The visions that swam in the air, and made hot

The breath of the north wind; the doubts and the hopes,
The terror and longing; and all through the whole
The feel of the deadly cold steel on the breast?
And the women—the horrid, sick dread in the blood
Of their smiles, of their voices, the touch of their hands,
The thrill of their garments against you: and then
The frenzy of fear lest the next that you met
Should be she; the taste in the air, on the tongue,
Of blood and of poison. And the shame!
Is it writ on the heavens or not? Is it spelled
On the pavement before you, or scrawled on the walls?
It is there, it is here, on the forehead, the hands,
In the blood, in the nostrils. And I loved her, I loved her,
Great Heaven! and did yet.

"This was anguish, you say.
Ah, you think so? For three months I lived in it, friend,
And then came despair, I had missed him—'twas done:
Let me be done, too. From the German frontier
Rose a clamor for soldiers. I heard, and grew calm.
'It is well,' I exclaimed. 'Men are shot in the field:
Let the enemy slay me.' So I came to the war."

He paused here a moment, and drew from his breast
A crumpled white paper streaked over with blood,
And laid it before me.

"You say this was anguish," he cried, "but I say
It was nothing—just nothing, My friend, can you think
What it were, or might be, if the woman you love—
Nay, nay, hear me out—should be playing above
The horrid steep side of a gulf, and you saw
Her footsteps draw nearer and nearer, and yet
Were too far to shriek warning; and at last as you looked,
Beheld her slip over—those eyes that you love,
The forehead, the hair—saw her struggle and catch
At some dizzy small branch that would hold but a breath,
And you yet afar? Can you think what it were
To hear her shriek out with assurance you'd heed
And would come, and that instant, while heaven and earth
Were one glare, and you rushed, to be caught, man, be caught
In a network of hell which you could not escape,
While she—she your heart's own—O death! yet is that
My soul-torment, look there!" and his shaking hand smoothed
The white paper before me. "Did you think she was false?
She was true, friend, was true; true as light, true as Heaven,
I have known it three hours. Was not false, was not base,
O my darling! my darling!

Beguiled, do you see—
Wooed away from my side with some smooth, hurried tale,

Till the length of the garden lay 'twixt us. Ah! ah!
Is there vengeance in hell for such villains? The rest?
You can guess how it happened—his sudden appeal—
The carriage—the horses—her cry which we heard not—
The rapid strong whirl of her head on his breast—
Then the rush and the night. Do you doubt it is true?
It is all written here. See the tremulous lines
How they cross and recross. But she's true; 'tis enough,
Four whole months and yet true. She has sworn it, and now
Do you see all my anguish?"

With hand and with voice
I strove in my pity to calm him: but he,
Staggering backward, went on: " 'Tis not all: she is held
In his power by his spies; he would wed her —great Heaven!
Make her countess or something; just stab her, I say!
And she calls me, entreats me, by all I adore,
To come quick, for she slips to destruction. Ha! ha!"
And his awful laugh whirled on the night-wind; "Come quick!
And I'm bound."

"How it came to this spot—when, I know not.
It was put in my hands as I strode from the field,
By some one who cried, 'If you hasten, perhaps
You have time still to save her.' Away to the chief
I hurried, a madman. What was France to me now,
Or the world? I fell down at his feet in despair;
Told him all; showed my billet—in vain, all in vain!
And to-morrow's the day of the battle!"

As in that
He had touched the whole depth of his woe, he flung up
His arms to the sky for a moment, and then
Sank down like one shot. When I rose from his side,
The dread morn of battle flamed high in the East.

Do you ask me for more? Lift the end of that cloth,
And behold! It is calm now, you see, sirs, quite calm—
'Twas not so yester eve. As he fell, all the din
Of the battle served not to o'erwhelm from my ears
The shriek that he gave.

Ode To France

January, 1871

   Land of mirth and dance,
      Fair pleasure-seeking France!
France of the laughing lip and careless eye!

Where is the lamp to light
Thy footsteps through the night
Now day has fled and darkness fills the sky?
What crown of hope remaineth now
The noontide flowers are dead upon thy chilling brow?

What strength hast thou to meet,
With unshod hurrying feet,
The rocky steeps and rugged paths of war?
Now that the fields are past,
The heavens overcast,
And north winds blow upon thee from afar?
What songs are left for thee to sing
Now that the timbrel's hushed and clarion trumpets ring?

Curse not the bitter hour!
After the full blown flower
Cometh the fruit; as sowing ye shall reap.
When bearded corn shall shoot
Up from the bramble's root,
And strength arise unshorn from sensual sleep,
Then from the head of less than Jove
Shall great Minerva spring and in full armor move.

Had ye no ears to hear
The mighty warning clear,
"Watch, for ye know not when the hour may come?"
Had ye no eyes to see
The small cloud's prophecy
Writ on the face of heaven's cerulean dome?
Was there no threatening shade forecast
Along thy sunny path from all the frowning past?

Didst think that God could brook
Upon thy sports to look
Forevermore nor stir upon His throne?
That through the measured beat
Of ceaseless dancing feet
No sounds arose in woeful undertone?
That slighted Sabbaths had no tongue
To plead within His ears, accusing crimes among?

The Justice which on high
Weighs all with nicety,
Hath weighed thy deeds, O trifling land of France!
In every cannon's word
His awful voice is heard;
By day and night his echoing steps advance;
Then fling thy gilded baubles down;
Who meekly bears the cross, shall wear the conquering crown.

Despair is not for thee!
What though thou bendest knee,
Whose crown once blazed in zenith pride on high!
So from thy present shame
Arise a nobler fame
As purest light athwart the deepest sky,
And from thy bended neck outspring
The strong and glowing plumes of Wisdom's soaring wing.

On The Threshold

Darling, why this dainty glow
Shifting on your cheeks of snow?
Why this look ok summer skies
Shining in your lifted eyes?

What new words are in the breeze?
What new whispers in the trees?
What soft language gently drips
From the roses' crimson lips;

That you wear so fresh a joy
In your smile's and glances coy;
That in every gesture fine
Such a wonderment should shine?

Hath the Spirit of all beauty
Kissed you in the path of duty;
Or that angel of the wood,
Holy-hearted Solitude?

Have you listened to the singing
Of the meadow-grasses springing?
Heard the shadows, whispering, tell
How they woo the asphodel?

Or has something yet more sweet,
Stranger yet and more complete,
Met you in the hidden ways
Trod by these fair autumn days?

Something lovely as the bright
Flushing of the morning light;
Something mystic as the free
Mighty, music-haunted sea?

Ah, my darling, ruby flush
O'er the snow cheek need not rush—
One can read the whole sweet story

In your brow's transparent glory.

Scents of violets crushed and sweet,
Halt about your pensive feet;
Golden glimmers gild your hair,
And you need not whisper where

You have wandered since I pressed
You in farewell to my breast;
Need not whisper that the snare
Caught your wild wings unaware.

Isabel Maynor

I sat with Philip 'neath his own roof-tree,
Watching his children sporting on the lea,
And half in pleasure at a scene so bright,
And half in envy of their young delight,
Uttered a sigh which all unconscious, he,
My well-loved friend repeated after me;
But in so doing hesitated not
To turn and ask what genius of the spot
Had filled my soul so full of bliss or woe,
A single breath could make it overflow.

"A man," I said, "possessed of every good
Which earth can lavish in her happiest mood;
A loving wife, a home where Pan might dwell
Forgetful of his flower-bespangled dell,
Can ask a houseless wanderer like me
In face of all this happiness I see,
What grief or joy can fill my spirit so,
A single breath can make it overflow."

"A houseless wanderer has but to wed,
To taste himself these vaunted sweets," he said;
"Fair women, friend, are not so scarce, I wot,
That one like you need mourn a lonely lot."
"Fair women, Philip," I returned, "bestrow
The world with smiles whichever way we go;
But ah, for me one fairest woman's face
Hath made me blind to every other's grace."

"Ah then, you love," he whispered; and a gray
Dull shadow fell upon his manner gay.
"But hold!" and flinging up the casement wide,
He sat again with forehead turned aside;
"As we are friends, you shall the whole recall
From her first smile to the blank end of all,

I am in mood to hear somewhat of grief,
Perhaps to set mine own joy in relief."

Bitter his smile, but sick of heart and worn
By a hard burden long in sorrow borne,
I only paused to cast one other glance
On those fair children in their mystic dance;
Then while their sweet tones trembled on the air
And mingled with my story unaware,
I told this tale of simple love and loss—
My daily memory and secret cross.

"Philip," I said, "far hence among the hills,
Where waves the birch and spring the mountain rills,
There stands a cottage whose four walls inclose
The sweetest maiden that this hard world knows.
Humble her home, but ah, the lowliest spot
May serve to hide the sweet forget-me-not;
The simplest glen that darkens in the woods,
Hold a shy moonbeam in its solitudes;
And Bella Maynor, though of humble birth.
Is fair to see as any flower of earth,
Ethereally pure, and full as bright
As softest moonbeam of a summer's night.

"It was by chance I found her; sweetest things
Come often thus, as from the welkin springs
The evening star when we but look to see
The stretch and shine of blue immensity,
I had been wandering 'neath a summer's sun
All day among the mountains with my gun,
When, stooping wearily above a stream,
I saw a shadow quivering in its gleam,
And glancing up, beheld her standing there
Against my side, with softly bashful air,
Offering a cup, and saying, I confess,
Words which I heard not for her loveliness.

"I took the cup; and, like the ocean shell
Which charmeth first by beauties visible,
She charmed that day, with lovely looks serene,
The tender harmony of face and mien;
But afterwards the music in the shell,
The sweetness of the soul made audible,
Grew on me and I vowed within my mind,
That she alone, of all fair womankind,
Should be mine own, and, by the name of wife,
Walk with me through the chance and change of life.

"But as the summer days and evenings passed,
Swift as a wind with music on the blast,

I found her brightest fancies were but flowers
Wreathed o'er the weariness of waiting hours.
She loved, I know not how the knowledge came
Unto me first—in coldness or in flame,
In gentle converse or abstracted look,
Beside the stream, or o'er some poet's book.
Enough that time the certain knowledge brought
She held a secret in her inmost thought;
A secret which in shyly hiding, she
Revealed to all around unconsciously;
As timid violets lade the ambient air
With their heart's richest fragrance, unaware
The fragrance whispers that the flower is there.

"But as the weeks fled by us and there came
No one across my pathway to reclaim
The hand I took at morn and evening light
With joyful greeting or too sad good night,
I 'gan to think her love was but a dream,
A star to fade in morning's fervent beam,
And mine alone the worship worth the while
Of that deep glance and shy, ecstatic smile;
And thinking thus, began to hope and blend
The reverent lover with the earnest friend.

"But ah, with the first hint of my desire,
She flashed one moment with indignant fire,
Then, slowly paling, told me that her faith
Was hers no more to grant this side of death;
And all unconscious of the light which lay
Upon her beauty in a vermeil ray,
Lifted her head and smiled, as if her eyes
Beheld afar the hills of Paradise.

"But I scarce waiting till the soft delight
Had flashed and faded from her forehead bright,
Bent to her ear and whispered, 'It is well,
But where is he who holds it, Isabel?
The summer comes; the tender summer goes;
The woods of Autumn blossom like the rose;
Winter descends; but he whose blessed right
It is to make your every season bright,
He only lingers; then as to a friend
Tell me in what far country he can wend,
Who holds in trust a heart so dear as this,
And yet can wander from his rightful bliss?'

"She did not answer, but her very frame
Seemed breathing forth a bright ethereal flame;
I felt the sudden splendor of her gaze
Surround and hold me like a summer's haze,

Yet could not quite forbear to say again,
'I would not doubt, but men are ever men,
And much I fear he may not love so well
As this pure trust deserveth, Isabel.'

"'His love to mine,' she answered through a blush
As tremulous as rose upon its bush,
'Is as the moon unto a timid star;
His shines, while mine but quivers from afar.
His love—it is as boundless as the sky,
And tender as the tear-drop in the eye,
As earnest as the sunlight upon earth,
As warm as leaping fire on the hearth.'

"'And yet—' I said. 'And yet,' she answered slow,
'You see no evidence of this, I know.
But ah, for me it lies within my heart;
It is enough for me to feel the start
Of mine own blood, to know that he is true,
Though all the world should fail, that he is true,
And will come yet to take unto his side
The humble mountain maiden for his bride,
That sooner than had doubted him, had died.'

"'Twas faith like that of saints for the dear Lord;
I felt my vain hopes perish at the word;
And bending o'er that sacred head, I took
 Her hand in mine with my last lover look.
'Bella,' I said, 'one word; but tell his name,
And I will trench no more upon his claim.'
And looking in my face she told it me
As one deals coin from golden treasury,
But telling, flushed, as if her tongue had given
To mortal ears what but belonged to heaven.

"But I, with reverence in my eye and soul,
Bent o'er her hand in lately learned control,
And praying God to bless her with His grace,
Went forth to hide the sorrow in my face;
Went forth to whisper to the brook and sky
The anguish of a love that could not die;
But which constrained me from that self-same day,
To seek in city street or mountain way,
The owner of the name I heard her say.

"But though for five long years I wandered wide
Through many a town, by many a fair hillside,
I have not found him, and my weary heart
Forgets not yet that moment's bitter smart;
Forgets not yet that form of tender grace,
The wild-flower loveliness of Bella's face,

Nor can forget till o'er life's fading hills
Descends the night that ends all human ills."

Softly I ceased; but he who sat beside
Rose to his feet and bending o'er me, cried,
"The name, what was it?" And half wonderingly,
I answered, "It was Philip, Philip Lee."
"And mine?" "And yours," I stammered under breath,
"Is Philip Morton." "Philip Lee," he saith.
"Lee Morton, friend; ah, ah you did not know,
Nor she, poor child, who loved and trusted so,
A man could wear half names beside the hearth
Of her he held the dearest upon earth!"

Then while I sat confused, o'ercome, dismayed,
He bowed his head upon his hands, and said,
"I meant not to deceive her; by my life
I loved her, would have made the child my wife;
But time and fashion, and the social use
Of moneyed men, the world and its abuse,
Came in between us, and you see the end—
For me, remorse; for her—thy sorrows, friend."

Myrna

When first I saw him, I but saw
    The shadow on his brow,
But, seeing that, forgot all else
    Of happiness or woe.

I had been plucking early bloom
    From where the brooklets run,
And stood just at the forest's verge,
    'Twixt shadow and the sun.

I am not fair like Maud and Jeanne,
    Nor gay like Clementine;
The glory lingering in their locks
    Forgets to brighten mine.

My footsteps pause amid the flowers
    They trample in their mirth;
For me a crown of mystic stars
    Lies on the breast of earth.

Yet as his eyes fell on my face,
    I saw his glance grow deep
As his who looks upon a lake
    Where moonbeams lie asleep.

And though his smile half passed away,
  'Twas like the fading light
Of stars that only fade because
  The dawn lifts on the night,

A maiden lovely as the first
  Arbutus-bloom of May,
Was with him when I next beheld
  Him pass along that way.

The boughs were waving o'er their heads,
  The sunbeams at their feet
Lay like half-woven coronals
  Of blossoms rare and sweet.

Yet when he came unto the spot
  Where I had stood that day,
I saw him pause and cast one glance
  Of wistfulness that way.

And seeing, I upraised my voice
  From out the woodland's heart,
And sang like one to whom the heavens
  Some vision fair impart.

I sang of stars—and straight the sky
  Seemed to grow still and dark,
And myriad burning jets of flame
  Shoot from it spark by spark.

I sang of bulbuls and the East—
  And through the woods there pressed
A thousand spicy scents that blew
  About my brow and breast.

And then, and then, like leaping flame
  My passionate soul upsprang,
I loosed my spirit on the world,
  And love, sweet love, I sang.

The birds were cooing in the trees,
  They grew as still as death;
The breeze that drinks the souls of flow'rs
  Paused on its perfumed breath.

And still I sang; like doom I sang;
  My soul arose in air;
I dropped the music from the clouds;
  I felt my face grow fair.

And when I ceased I saw afar,
  Toward the setting sun,
His head sink slowly on his breast,
  Like one whose race is run.

And though the mellow twilight soon,
  Like purple-breasted dove,
Passed flying towards the blazoned west
  And all was dark above,

I did not stir, but sat like one
  From whom the world has sped;
My eyes upon the way he went,
  The shadows on my head.

Alas, the days are long since then,
  And many an eve gone by,
But still in dreams I sit and watch
  That barren heath and sky.

Coming Home From The Fair

She thinks she is pretty—look there!
How she smiles in his face through her hair,
With a gleam in her eye like the star-drop you see
In a blossom half ope to the bee.

She thinks she is pretty—her cheeks
Have a dimple so sweet when she speaks,
And she wonders perchance as she leans on his arm
If I know or can guess all her charm.

She thinks that he loves her, perhap,
That the fairing he threw in her lap,
Had a story to tell if she chose for her part
To remember a moment her heart.

She thinks that he loves her, ah yes;
And laughs in the gay consciousness,
With a throb of delight that the brown eyes should bear
Such a treasure as this from the fair.

But ah, if she knew, if she knew
What he whispered but now to the blue,
With a thrill in his voice and a look that was worth
All she gets from his youth and his mirth;

How the eyes that look down are the sweetest,
As those flowers are the rarest, completest,

Which the hand must uplift ere the gazer can see
All the treasures they hide from the bee.

The Confession of The King's Musketeer

Confess! I will confess; but first as thou
Dost love thine holy office, rise and look
From yonder grating opening on the bay,
And tell me—for my chains drag heavily—
If far away where sky and billow meet,
You see a scarlet pennon floating free.
Yes? then draw near and I will tell you all
As if within a true confessional,
Contented thus to speak the truth and die.

She was a dream to me, a gentle zephyr
Stealing across the fever of my life,
Sweet with all soothing fragrance; halting not,
But leaving in my ears, in fluttering by,
The wild sweet music of the birds and brooks,
Within my breast, the freshness of the summer.
I loved her, if men call it love to give
Their soul in worship to a star of heaven;
But whatso'er you think—and holy men
Will have their thoughts—for all my love and worship,
I was not wont to gaze upon her much,
Not much, though every lineament of hers
Was precious unto me as mine own soul.

She was my lord king's daughter, heir to crowns
And wearer of the purple from her birth,
While I—I was a simple musketeer,
A sword to be drawn freely in her cause,
But not to be wide brandished in her sight
Unless the hour demanded. Wherefore then
These chains, the gallows lifted in the court,
And all yon preparation for stem death?
Was I not found before her on my knees
Within the sacred precincts of her room?
I was.
              But ere I lift the veil too high,
Look out once more and by the Christ you worship,
Tell me if yonder pennon which you see,
Holds on its course unstayed across the bay.
Yes? It is well; then listen.

For a year
I held my station close against her door,
And heard her steps go by me morn and night,

And never raised an eyelid. But one day,
Just as she turned to glide adown the hall,
An impulse seized me like a stormy wind
To gaze upon the beauty which had been
My dream from early youth. But when, with just
One quick upgathering of my soul like that
With which a man dares flood or braves the fire,
I raised mine eyes and looked upon her face,
I did not see its beauty, did not feel
Its bright consummate charm of glance and smile,
Not then, not then; for, fainter than the shade
Which falls from heaven's fleeciest summer-cloud
Upon a swaying oleander-bud,
And melts away again ev'n while you wonder
If 'tis a shadow or the blossom's richness,
A mist lay o'er its lustre, and mine eyes
Saw but that mist, no more. And though, ere long,
She flitted from my side all gaiety,
I could not sleep my natural sleep that night.
For thinking of the veil of grief or care
Which lay so faintly on her loveliness

But when, as week joined week I heard her step,
Drag slowlier and slowlier down the hall,
And the delicious murmur of her laugh
Fall faintlier and faintlier on the ear,
My heart turned cold within me. Was it death?
Or marking how the gallants of the court
Crowded like moths of summer at her coming,
That evil worse than death, a hopeless love,
Laying a hand of ice upon my heart
I bent myself to watch. But although earth
Had lent her noblest, loftiest, and best
To make our court the stateliest in the world,
And gallants were as plenty as the pearls
Upon the royal diadem, she passed
Among them all as smiling and serene
As the high moon amid the clouds of even.
"It is not love," I said, "it must be death."

But on the morrow as I stood and watched
With heavy gaze the self-same crowd go by,
A quick form brushed me and a blossom fell
As from a restless hand against my foot,
And looking up, I saw the Count di Ferra
Turn for an instant from the crowd and fix
His eyes in wild entreaty upon mine.
Next moment, stealing on me like a ray
Of faintest moonlight through a prison's gloom,
I spied my royal princess. I could hear
Her breath come, go, painting alternately

Glad rose and fearful lily on her cheek,
And scarcely knowing what it was I did,
I stooped and raised the blossom from the ground,
And kneeling, dropped it in her open palm.
She took it; for a moment earth and heaven
Swam in one whirl about me, then a calm
Fell on my spirit, and I slowly rose,
Knowing as if an angel had proclaimed it,
That soon or late, on that day or another,
My life would follow in the blossom's wake.

Then was it that each morning at the dawn
I looked upon the sun in its first splendor
As one who questions, "What hast thou for me?"
And every evening as that splendor paled,
And ghastly as a spirit from the grave,
The wild moon rose upon me, "What hast thou?"
Preparing thus my soul against the day,
When he should fling the flower of my life
Beneath her feet, and she should lean to take it.

At last it came. I had been at my post
Since heavy noon, and I was wondering why
The princess so delayed to venture forth,
When suddenly from where the fountains play
Down in the court, there broke upon my ears
A short, sharp cry, "Stand by there for your lives,
And let no one pass by on pain of death!"
It was the king's voice; but before mine eyes
Could turn within their sockets, the closed door
Which guarded the young princess from the world,
Swung on its noiseless hinges, and her face,
Awful in high devotion and despair,
Looked out and brightened on me like a star,
Then grew as fixed as death. "I want," she said—
And low as were the words they filled mine ears
And fell upon my breast like dropping ice,

"The help of one who for my sake will brave
The shame and terror of a bitter death."

I did not tremble. Earth's most awful joys
Make men quite calm. Giving her look for look,
But stopping not for any mock of words,
I followed and stepped in and shut the door,
And heard it clang behind me. Then, O then,
The usage of my thoughts passed quite away,
And what she was and what I was, I lost
In the great splendor which her beauty made
Through all the room. I had no need to turn
My head to know whose form it was that stood

Behind me. In her eyes his image burned,
And down through every fibre of her frame
The fervor and the purpose of a love
That dares all things, fears nought and devotes all,
Flashed like a flame.

      "Madame," I cried, "your will!
Let me but know your will!"

      "First hear my need."
And looking up, she cried below her breath,
"I love the Count di Ferra; he is here:
We were to have been wedded ere the eve,
But some one has betrayed us. At the door
The king stands; in the court beneath us there,
Await three soldiers ready with drawn swords
To smite whoever leaps from out the casement;
Protect him! but first slay me where I stand,
That he, my father, seeing me lie low,
May stop to mourn and give him chance to fly."
And flinging all her beauty to the ground,
She knelt, my princess, knelt before my feet.

But I, scarce waiting for the smile she strove
To give me for a guerdon, for the sound
Of his quick passionate voice in wild disclaim,
Asked if men knew her lover. And she said,
"None on God's earth save we." Whereat at once
A great light spread itself within my soul,
And bidding her to thrust him out of sight,
I raised mine eyes and looked upon her face
For the last time on earth.

      Madam," I said,
"I love you. I have loved you all my life;
A musketeer has loved you all his life;
'Tis meet for such offence that he should die.
But you, remember you this thing and live.
That on the morrow at the hour of noon,
From out the port below us in the bay,
There sails a bark unto the shores of Greece,
 Guided by men I know. Now if so be
That all goes well, and you and he with faith
Fast wedded by some holy man of God,
Have gained a refuge in the little craft,
Uplift a scarlet pennon at the bow,
And let it float till out of sight of land.
Remember."

      Waiting not to see the look
Of startled wonder ebb from out her eyes,

I knelt and took her robe within my hands
And kissed it, just as through the opening door,
The king leaped in upon us. How he sprang
Like flame upon my throat, and how she swooned
Protesting wildly in my innocence,
It boots not now to tell. Enough that I
Was deemed by him her lover and immured
Within these dungeon walls, before her eyes
Had oped again unto the light of day.
But he was saved! and now I ask no more
But that yon scarlet pennon on the sea,
Sink from the wide horizon and be lost,
The hour I give my parting breath to heaven.

His wish was granted. As the prison guns
Proclaimed to all the world the deed was done,
The little flag, that for so long a time
Had fluttered on the bosom of the bay,
Trembled from sight across the far horizon.

What Do The Roses Say In Their Dreams?
WHAT do the roses say in their dreams?
    Let us hark and hear! Let us hark and hear!
Do they echo the songs of the eager streams,
    Running so near, running so clear?
Or have they a murmur of love and fear
    For the bliss of the wandering breeze's ear?

Do they murmur of skies and the longing stars?
    Let us hark and hear! Let us hark and hear!
Are their rich hearts full of the glory of Mars,
    With his blood red shield, and his golden spear?
Or doth the thought of some softer sphere
    Well up from their depths in a tremulous tear?

I would know! I would know! How they tremble and burn!
    Hark, then, and hear! Hark, Love, and hear!
By the stir at their hearts we shall surely learn
    In an instant now what hope or fear,
What rapture or pain, what sorrow or cheer
    Thrills through the breast of each beauty here.

Then, Love, stoop close, No rosier bud
    Doth nestle here than thy rose ear.
Stoop close! Such beauty can ne'er intrude.
    And now what is it they say, my dear?
You blush, Sweet-heart. Ah! did'st thou fear
    Aught else but thine own name to hear?

A Legend of Antwerp

They led him forth. The morning sun
    Was shining wide o'er field and rill;
The glory of a day begun
    Was in the sky, was on the hill,
    Was in the wild bird's early trill.

His form was high, his cheek was fair,
    The star of youth was on his brow,
The shadow of his falling hair
    Was turning, in the early glow,
    To the clear sunshine's rippling flow.

They led him forth. They bade him look
    His very last upon the day,
And from his eyes the bandage took
    One moment, that the morning's ray
    Might bless him ere he passed away.

He looked around. He looked above,
    On purple mount and tender sky.
Then turned and gazed on human love,
    In sweet girl faces hurrying by,
    And bowed his noble head to die.

When lo! from out the heaving throng
    Behold a sudden form appear!
Ethereal as a dreaming song
    Stealing through fragrant groves to cheer
    The restless spirit of the ear.

A girlish form, so mystic bright,
    The very guards were touched by fear
And trembled backward as the light
    Of her pure glance fell on them, clear
    As moonlight shimmering on the mere.

He shall not die, she said, and laid
    Her woman's hand upon his breast,
Her bright smile glowing undismayed
    From out her locks, as from the west
    Looks forth a young star's joyful crest

And such, the legend runs, her grace,
    And such the power of her mien,
She seemed to fill the market-place
    With sense of angel forms serene
    And sound of harps that sang unseen.

He shall not die! and from the crowd

She led him forth, while heavenly awe
Fell on each wondering heart, and bowed
   The head of every mortal there,
   Filling the silence like a prayer.

She led him forth, and none might say
   If earth or Heaven was in the power
Of that young maiden's love that day,
   To still the passions of the hour
   And baffle vengeance in its flower.

We only know they passed unharmed
   By peasant's cot and noble's hall.
And, in their youth and beauty armed,
   Sped scathless through the city's wall
   And vanished from the sight of all.

Sunrise From The Mountains

Hung thick with jets of burning gold, the sky
Crowns with its glorious dome the sleeping earth,
Illuminating hill and vale. O'erhead,
The nebulous splendor of the milky way
Stretches afar; while, crowding up the heavens,
The planets worship 'fore the throne of God,
Casting their crowns of gold beneath His feet.
It is a scene refulgent! and the very stars
Tremble above, as though the voice divine
Reverberated through the dread expanse.
But soft! a change!
A timid creeping up of gray in east—
A loss of stars on the horizon's verge—
Gray fades to pearl and spreads-up zenithward,
The while a wind runs low from hill to hill,
As if to stir the birds awake, rouse up
The nodding trees, and draw off silence like
A garment from the drowsy earth. The heavens
Are full of points of light that go and come
And go, and leave a tender ashy sky.
The pearl has pushed its way to north and south,
Save where a line spun 'tween two peaks at east,
Gleams like a cobweb silvered by the sun.
It grows—a gilded cable binding hill
To hill! it widens to a dazzling belt
Half circling earth, then stretches up on high—
A golden cloth laid down 'fore kingly feet.

Thus spreads the light upon the heavens above.
While earth hails each advancing step, and lifts

Clear into view her rich empurpled hills,
To keep at even beauty with the sky.
The neutral tints are deeply saffroned now;
In streaks, auroral beams of colored light
Shoot up and play about the long straight clouds
And flood the earth in seas of crimson. Ah,
A thrill of light in serpentine, quick waves,
A stooping of the eager clouds, and lo,
Majestic, lordly, blinding bright, the sun
Spans the horizon with its rim of fire!

Separated

When in the solemn dusk you sit and think,
With face upturned to the enduring skies,
Of life and art, and those great griefs that sink
The soul in woe in spite of high emprise—
I know not how, but from the surging sea
Of these thy thoughts, some echo comes to me,
Moving my soul till from its billows rise
The answering strain for which thy spirit cries,
And then, or joy, or sorrow holds the throne
Of thy strong heart, thou art no more alone.

The Barricade

One in a million? True, sir, true;
    Nor is it strange you marvel so
To see such eyes look down on you
    From walls so barren, mean and low.
But 'tis my only daughter's face,
        For all the grace
Of the rich beauty that you see;
And where, then, where a fitter place
For her to smile, than here on me,
Who nourished her in infancy!

One in a million! So was said
    By many a one that, riding by,
Beheld her lovely bended head
    Between them and the summer sky.
She wore so grand a look, you see,
        Unconsciously;
A lily musing in a beam
Of starlight, were as apt as she
To turn aside and fondly dream
Of its own shadow in the stream.

She was so true. Ah, when by chance
　　I seem again her form to see,
It is not she who died for France,
　　That rises to my memory;
But the dear girl who sat of yore
　　　　Within my door,
Reeling her thread by night and day,
Contented, though the breezes bore
Up from the meadows strown with hay,
The sound of merry youth at play.

Too bright for such a doom? Ah sir,
　　Her very brightness hid a tear;
I scarce could ever look at her
　　Without a sigh of love and fear.
Such sacred stillness seemed enshrined
　　　　Deep in her mind;
The stillness of a soul that knows
A trumpet call is on the wind
That unto others, only blows
The careless perfume of the rose.

What was her story? Is it not
　　Then, written in those eyes of hers?
Glances so deep and sad, I wot,
　　Should be their own interpreters.
Yet may there linger unaware
　　　　Beneath that tear,
The tokens of another's smart,
As oft in sweetest rhymes you hear
Beneath the language of his art,
The beatings of the poet's heart.

For he who limned those features, sir,
　　Had loved her once; poor Jean Vigny!
He died, they say, in blessing her,
　　Upon the field of Champigny.
A generous youth in all was he,
　　　　And true; but she
Absorbed in girlish fancies bright,
Walked in his smile, serenely free,
Unknowing that its genial light
Sprang from the depths of darkest night.

Perchance it was that he had been
　　Her play-fellow from earliest youth,
And that there was no mystery in
　　His honest glance of love and truth,
But this I know, that one fair day
　　　　In early May,

He left us to return no more.
I saw him as he moved away,
Pause softly in the open door,
And bless the threshold o'er and o'er.

Next morn he came. Why is it now,
   Remembering all as it befell,
I yet can bless the transient glow
   Which led him to our humble well?
He was so noble, sir, to see;
        Such majesty
Was in his mien and bearing bold:
My very cup took dignity
Beneath his glance which gently told
'Twas welcome as a cup of gold.

He quaffed, and in a moment more
   Had passed forever from my sight,
Had not the linnet at the door,
   Upraised a song of such delight,
He turned—Ah, on what simple things
        Our future swings;
What wondrous issues hang upon
The idle song a linnet sings!
He turned, and there, where roses run
Saw Clarice standing in the sun.

With one meek hand upon her breast,
   The other clinging to the vine,
She stood in her young beauty dressed
   As in a robe of golden shine.
I saw him start; I saw the blush
        Of manhood flush
Responsive to that vision bright,
And turning, let my whole soul rush
In love and fear, to hail the sight
Of her young innocent delight.

But ah, in that uplifted face
   No answering color met my view,
A mortal in her winning grace,
   She seemed a trancèd spirit too
I felt a stinging terror dart
        Keen through my heart,
As I beheld that raptured eye,
And marked the reckless blood-drops start
Unheeded from her hand, and dye
The thorns she grasped unconsciously.

He saw, and gently laid his hand
   Upon the bridle of his steed,

That, faithful to his least command,
   Paced slowly onward down the mead.
I marked him leaning backward still,
     As o'er the hill
He passed and vanished in the wood;
And turning with a nameless thrill
To clasp my darling where she stood,
Found silence there and solitude.

But when at eventide I drew
   Her face to mine with fond good night,
No lurking shadow met my view
   Commingled with its wonted light;
Rather a shyly added gleam,
     As though some dream
Had brushed her by with ardent wing;
Some mellow sunset loosed its beam
Upon a wave yet fluttering
With ecstasy of early spring.

"Is it that he will come again?"
   I asked and sighed; "or do some souls,
Like the deep sea-shell, catch one strain
   Of the world's music as it rolls,
And tranced in wonder and delight,
     Fold up their bright
Warm walls about it evermore;
Content to whisper day and night,
By land and sea, the echo o'er
Of that one instant's joy and power."

I dared not think. Meantime the spring
   Cast by her veil of amber mist,
And in full splendor stopped to ring
   The lilac boughs with amethyst,
Methinks the world was ne'er so fair;
     The very air
Hung poised as if on golden wings;
A light like love was everywhere,
And yet for me, the fear of things
Unknown, made dim earth's blossomings.

But one clear day in early June
   As I sat busy at my wheel,
Crooning perhaps an old time tune
   Of lover's woe or 'over's weal,
I felt the shadow and the gloom
     Of that small room
Yield to a sudden burst of light,
And glancing with a sense of doom
Toward the door, beheld her bright,

Full figure lifted to its height.

O never, never till I die
   Shall I forget the look she wore,
As gazing on me silently
   She crossed the sunny, sanded floor.
It was as if a regal crown
      Had settled down
Upon the artless brow I knew;
Her very step, her simple gown,
Transfigured in its lustre, grew
In dignity beneath my view.

"Mother—" and at the word her smile
   Passed softly in a roseate bloom,
As sinks the sun away, the while
   All heaven flowers in its room—
"There's one without awaits the cheer
      Of welcome here;
Speak to him for I go,"' she said;
And even while I faltered near,
Drooped lower, lower yet her head,
And vanished with reluctant tread.

That instant through the swaying vines
   He proudly stepped. O lover eyes!
O lover brows! how brightly shines
   The sun of hope in youthful skies!
My old heart trembled as I gazed,
      My eyeballs dazed;
I seemed as by some vision's stress
To see that other go dispraised,
That yet in going stopped to bless
The threshold he no more would press.

But strong in might of motherhood
   To save my child from loss and woe,
I moved and faced him where he stood,
   With quivering lip but steady brow.
"Fair sir," I said, "in careless hour
      A wild-wood flower
May seem a treasure to the eye,
But place it in a lady's bower,
And what was radiant 'neath the sky
Seems only fit to fade and die."

" 'Tis true," he cried, "but lady's bower
   And a man's earnest heart are twain:
Sheltered by love, no stormy shower
   Shall reach thy wilding sweet, again."
Then while I slowly shook my head,

He softly said,
"Thou hast a mother's constancy;
I have no mother; when I wed,
The mother of my wife must be
A mother also unto me."

I turned away. I could not speak;
    Like shadows on a moonlit stream,
I felt my thoughts confusing break
    Across an underlying gleam.
A moment more, and through the flush
        Of vine and bush
I saw him pass unto her side;
Then all grew dark, and a great gush
Of music swam up on the wide,
Swift breeze that filled the mountain side.

Why need I linger? Ere the week
    Had passed in all its cheer away,
The April of my darling's cheek
    Had bloomed and budded like the May.
She had no need of speech to tell
        What fairy bell
Had rung its summons in her soul;
The lips which smiled, the lids which fell,
The brow's transparent aureole,
Unwittingly revealed the whole.

You see she was a maiden, sir,
    That till that time had never known
What 'twas to have another stir
    The current of life's undertone.
The falling shadows in the woods'
        Deep solitudes,
My mother glance, the sudden flow
Of waters in the mountain floods,
Had moved her, but such passion, no;
'Twas sunlight falling upon snow.

My darling loved, then; but for such,
    Grief follows love as night the day;
And all this joy was but the touch
    Of rapture ere it fled away;
The last, soft glimmer of the blue
        Of heaven through
The gathering rush of hurrying cloud;
The final welling up of dew
Upon the blossom ere it bowed
Before the fierce destroyer proud.

But ere the Sunday eve had come,

The ringing trump of war had blown
Across the threshold of our home,
  And he who held her dear had gone.
Gone, gone, and she, pure heart, was left
      Behind, bereft
Ere love's first week had run its sands;
Her thread of hope by stem fate, cleft
While yet its silver shining strands
Gleamed bright and beauteous in her hands.

My child, my child! But she like one
  Who sees beyond the deep abyss,
A country flowering in the sun,
  All luminous with love and bliss,
Lost not that look which was my joy,
      But in the coy
Delight of memory found a spell
The present grief could not destroy;
The eyes o'erhung with asphodel,
Saw not the shade that round her fell.

But as the days fled by, and sounds
  Of warfare mingled with the blast,
And nearer, nearer to our bounds
  The frowning shade of Battle passed;
As death and danger filled the air,
      And many a fair
Fond woman's countenance showed trace
Of wasting grief or anxious care,
I marked upon my darling's face,
Another look find gradual place.

A new, strange look, not terror, no,
  Nor anguish, no, nor fear for him;
But something subtiler, such a glow
  As a quick torch swung through the grim,
Dead darkness of the midnight air,
      Might cause to flare
Upon the placid, marble brow
Of some sweet Mary, gleaming fair
From wayside shrine upon the woe
Of a lost wanderer down below.

A look that froze me, warmed me, dazed
  And would not leave my dreams at night;
A look that deepened as I gazed,
  And filled my soul with vague affright.
"Alas," I cried, "she hears afar
      The voice of war;
She will not linger long away;
The sound of battle in her ear

Is like a call she must obey:"
But O the love, the heart's dismay!

And I was right; another week
　　And we had left our home behind,
In Paris' surging streets to seek
　　The work for which her spirit pined.
"I could not live so far," she said,
　　　　"From where his head
May come some weary day to lie;
Nor breathe my breath and know some bed
Of pain was comfortless, that I
Might ease perhaps with smile or sigh.

"I am at rest now," and she turned
　　Her face in glad content on mine,
Through whose pure light her glances burned
　　Like holy lamps on holy shrine.
"The smile I may not give to him
　　　　Need not grow dim
While pain and sorrow plead for aid;
The eyes he loved, forget to brim
With pity, or the heart he made
His own, grow faint with hopes delayed."

And clad with this strong hope, she grew
　　At once so beautiful and bright,
She seemed like one on whom some new
　　Fair world had opened in delight.
For me it was enough to see
　　　　The helpful, free,
Sweet way of her in all distress;
To hear her voice, and know that she
Was happy, and that pain was less,
And sorrow, for that happiness.

But what say I? 'Tis not of this
　　Our conflict with the foreign foe,
That I would speak to-day—it is
　　Of her and of our final woe.
And she was in no peril then,
　　　　Not even when
Gaunt Famine stalked the city through,
And women sickened, yes, and men
Lay down to die within our view,
And want was as the breath we drew.

It is of that dread after-hour
　　When passion oped the door of hell,
And glutting fury rose to power,
　　And might was lord, that I would tell.

O awful flame of burning homes!
      Of falling domes!
Against your scarlet tapestry,
One figure only goes and comes
Whene'er I look, one only, see
How angel-like it smiles on me!

But to my story. France had bowed
   Her haughty head unto her fate,
And the last Prussian's footstep proud
   Had echoed through our city's gate:
And peace was ours at last, if not
      The happier lot
Of conquerors in their victory;
The last fierce cannon had been shot,
And life and love were safe, and he
Our hero; priceless treasury.

To me no other thought was worth
   The tribute of a passing sigh;
I could have carolled in my mirth,
   That day of shame and misery.
But ah, it was not so with her;
      For all the stir
Of hope upspringing in her breast,
A shadow like the dreamy blur
That veils the moon, lay half confessed
Upon her beauty's glowing crest.

And when I cried, "A happy day
   Is this which sees the Prussians gone,
So happy, this dear forehead may
   Soon wear, perhaps, its marriage crown,
She did not make me quick reply,
      But dropped her eye
And shuddered faintly like a flower
That feels the wind go chilling by,
Though all things else around and o'er
Hang still nor own its artful power.

"A happy day, but—" and her gaze
   Passed quickly to the open door—
"It is upon life's sunniest days
   The storm prepares that whelms us o'er."
O what was it that smote my heart?
      What stinging dart
Of terror, menace, doubt or woe
Was hidden in those words apart,
That all my life-blood ceased to flow
In peace, as she thus murmured low?

Moving aside, I raised my eyes
   To where her glance had sped before,
When what was that which hid the skies
   Just shining through the open door?
A face, but ah, how dread, how rude
     In its wild mood!
If it had been a tiger's own,
I had not sprung from where I stood
With fiercer cry, nor quicker thrown
My arms round Clarice standing lone.

And yet it was a manly face
   Which some fond mother's lips had kissed,
A countenance where thought had place—
   The thought though of a dogmatist.
I did not know him then by name,
     But through the flame
Of the fell glance which sought, alas!
My daughter's face with passionate claim,
I seemed to see as in a glass
The spirit of a demon pass.

And though in just a moment more
   He vanished even while I looked,
And heaven's pure sky all sunnied o'er
   Came shining inward unrebuked,
I could not choose but feel the gloom
     Of some near doom
Had fallen about us unaware;
A breath, a whisper from the tomb
Had crossed our summer garden fair,
Leaving its poison in the air.

But hiding in my mother breast
   The terror I could not repress,
I strove with merry smiles and jest
   To win her back to happiness.
But she who ever until now
     Had raised her brow,
Serene amid the darkest hour,
Drooped slowly from this time as though
She felt a blight upon the flower
Of her young life and maiden power.

But not until that fearful day
   He came again and with some word
Of love and love's resistless sway,
   Strove hard to make his passion heard;
Not till commanded from her sight,
     He turned his bright
Fierce gaze on us and bade us know

By the low sounds of restless fight
Just waking in the streets below,
That will was law in Paris now:

Did I foresee that we were lost,
    If Victor came not soon to aid.
That the shy leaf by zephyrs tossed,
    Was to the whirlwind's grasp betrayed,
But Victor could not come, the toils
        With tightening coils
Had caught us in their fatal snare;
The frantic freedom which despoils
And heedeth nought, was in the air,
And cannon's voice mocked every prayer.

And as the conflict round us grew
    Intenser in its frenzy dire,
He fiercer turned as though he drew
    Fresh fury from each mounting fire.
"Thou art my bride," he used to say;
        "And sharest sway
With freedom in this breast of mine;
Your fates are one; the self-same day
That sees her fall, sees thee and thine
Laid bruised and bleeding on her shrine."

And when the hours in flying brought
    The deadly struggle to a head,
And wild despair and passion sought
    To do the work of hope, now dead,
It was no raging man that came
        Red from the flame
To gloat a moment o'er his power,
But some mad demon dead to shame,
That in his frenzy found an hour
To tread and break a wilding flower:

My innocent child! But she with calm,
    High aspect kept him still at bay,
And with one name as with a charm,
    Stayed up her courage night and day.
Meantime about our very door
        The rush and roar
Of warfare 'gan to ebb and swell,
And barricades arose before
Our eyes, and nearer, deadlier, fell
The hissing shot and bursting shell.

And listening to their sullen call,
    And looking on their angry glare,
I could but pray their wrath might fall

Upon us twain in our despair,
But she at that would whisper "Nay,
        O rather pray
That you may live though Clarice die;
If but upon some happier day
To tell my Victor, how that I
Was true unto life's latest sigh."

And leaning on my mother breast,
    She raised her earnest face to mine
And murmured, "Death for me is best,
    You must not grieve at God's design."
Then as I shuddered, added slow:
        "The noon-day glow
Of life had been too bright for me;
I was not made to stem the flow
Of daily care, nor live to see
My dreams fade in reality.

"To live, to love and then to die
    While life and love are pure and sweet
As April's mingled smile and sigh
    In which all hopeful fancies meet,
Is not so sad; more sad to me,
        It were to see
The falling leaves, the clouding sky,
To look around and miss the free
Glad singing of the birds, and sigh
In vain for hopes and days gone by.

"A mist just blown from off the hills
    Across the roses of the dawn,
That for a moment burns and thrills,
    With splendor from their glory drawn;
It were not meet for me to scale—
        A thing so frail—
The lofty facade of the sky,
Nor made to shimmer and to fail,
Bear up my heart as though my way
Lay through the golden ranks of day.

"Even the love which God has given
    To make my summer morn complete,
Is more a thing of happy heaven
    Than happy earth, however sweet.
And he will say so, too, at last
        When all is passed
And life resumes its wonted calm;
'Tis not for one like me to cast
My lot with such as he; the balm
Is sweet, but mates not with the palm.

"Yet does he love me; meek, untaught,
    And tender as all meek things be,
I know he holds me high as aught
    That blooms or gleams on land or sea.
And I would ever shine thus bright
        Within his sight;
And if I die it will be so,
For Death's deep portals shed a light
On the dear ones who pass below,
That shrines them in enduring glow

"And thus in fair, eternal youth,
    With cheek undimmed and smile unworn,
With eyes that never lose their truth,
    And lips whose speech is ne'er forsworn,
I'll walk beside him day by day,
        Life's long hard way;
His hope in sorrow or despite,
But in his joy a memory;
As stars shine o'er us, dim or bright,
As beams the morn or glooms the night."

Pausing, she stood with lifted head
    Turned towards that fiery booming sky,
Serene, though death and anguish sped
    In every shot that hurried by.
When, hark! from where the noise and glare
        Seethe up the stair,
A sudden flash, a frenzied cry!
And awful in his wild despair,
That demon fronts us with the high,
Red flame of conflict in his eye.

Ah, God of grace! But with a bound
    He caught her form from off the floor,
And shrieking out, "The end is found!"
    Fled with her through the open door.
I heard his footsteps as they rung,
        The shriek she flung
To Heaven in her extremity,
And rousing, tottering upward, sprung
Along their wake, while under me
The earth rose heaving like the sea.

Down, down the stair that shook beneath,
    Across the landing, out the gate,
And forth into the flaming death,
    Fled like a mad thing to my fate.
A bullet struck me as I passed,
        A fiery blast

Swept by me, scathing cheek and brow,
But heedless, reckless, onward, fast
As doom itself, I rushed, nor knew
I crushed the dying as I flew.

They told me later that it was
    The very crisis of the fight;
That even as I strove to pass,
    The barricade fell from its height.
But I saw not; my gaze, my all
        Was on that small
Frail figure flying from my eyes,
Borne on through flame, past rushing ball,
Up, up, unto the topmost rise
Of those wild ruins 'gainst the skies.

But stunned and deafened as I was,
    The silence which fell on the fray,
As forth upon that tottering mass
    He leaped with her, and stood at bay,
Is with me yet; as if a flood
        On rushing, should
In one wild moment fall backthrown—
The very life chilled in the blood,
And when he spake his words rang lone,
As through some wilderness of stone.

"Ha, slaves! and will you falter now?"
    I heard him shriek with frenzied cry.
"Now when fair Freedom waits your blow
    To bow her radiant head and die?
We do not falter," and he drew
        His blade and threw
One frantic glance on Clarice's brow;
"Never! Then come." And into view
Raising his threatening arm, stood so
With maddened eye bent on the foe.

When hark, beneath, around, above,
    A hurried cry, "On, comrades, on!
He holds them back, they dare not move,
    Their leader seemeth turned to stone;
Vive la Commune!" And with a bound
        That shook the ground,
A dozen threatening forms rushed by.
I heard, threw off my gathering swound,
Looked, saw in that same leader's eye
Our Victor's tortured soul flash high.

She sees him too, and o'er her falls
    A sudden light. "Ah, Heaven," she cries,

"Do Frenchmen pause when duty calls
  Because a single French girl dies?
Rouse,Victor, rouse!" But stunned, dismayed,
      He only swayed
One restless moment towards the strife:
I saw her tremble, look for aid,
Grow firm, then smile, and crying, "Life
For honor!" spring to meet the knife.

The charm was broken. With a yell
  That demon flung her to the ground,
And in the sudden tumult, hell
  Itself seemed bursting from its bound.
But life and death were now to me
      As equal; she
The beautiful, the fond, the dear,
Had perished, and not ev'n the cry
Of Victor in his grief could e'er
Rouse me again to wrath or fear.

Anna Katharine Green -- A Concise Bibliography

The Leavenworth Case (1878)
A Strange Disappearance (1880)
The Sword of Damocles: A Story of New York Life (1881)
The Defence of the Bride, and other Poems (1882)
X Y Z: A Detective Story (1883)
Hand and Ring (1883)
The Mill Mystery (1886)
7 to 12: A Detective Story (1887)
Risifi's Daughter, A Drama (1887)
Behind Closed Doors (1888)
Forsaken Inn (1890)
A Matter of Millions (1891)
The Old Stone House and Other Stories (1891)
Cynthia Wakeham's Money (1892)
Marked "Personal" (1893)
Miss Hurd: An Enigma (1894)
The Doctor, His Wife, and the Clock (1895)
Doctor Izard (1895)
That Affair Next Door (1897)
Lost Man's Lane: A Second Episode in the Life of Amelia Butterworth (1898)
Agatha Webb (1899)
The Circular Study (1900)
A Difficult Problem (1900)
One of my Sons (1901)
The Filigree Ball: Being a Full and True Account of the Solution of the Mystery Concerning the Jeffrey-Moore Affair (1903)
The Amethyst Box (1905)

The House in the Mist (1905)
The Millionaire Baby (1905)
The Chief Legatee' (1906)
The Woman in the Alcove (1906)
The Mayor's Wife (1907)
The House of the Whispering Pines (1910)
Three Thousand Dollars (1910)
Initials Only (1911)
Masterpieces of Mystery (1913)
Dark Hollow (1914)
The Golden Slipper, and Other Problems for Violet Strange (1915)
To the Minute; Scarlet and Black: Two Tales of Life's Perplexities (1916)
The Mystery of the Hasty Arrow (1917)
The Step on the Stair (1923)

www.ingramcontent.com/pod-product-compliance
Lightning Source LLC
Chambersburg PA
CBHW060143050426
42448CB00010B/2277